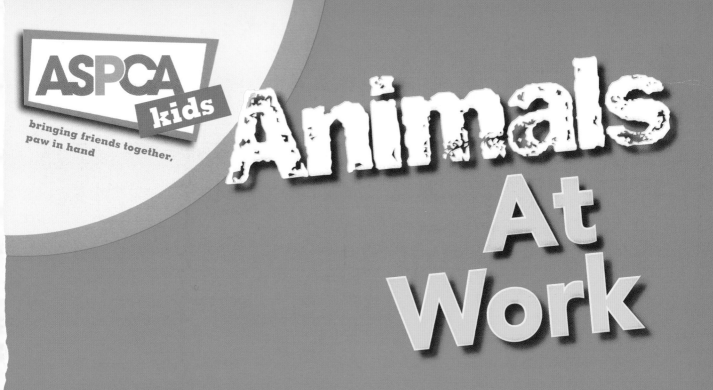

ASPCA **kids**

bringing friends together, paw in hand

Animals At Work

Liz Palika
Dr. Katherine A. Miller

WILEY
Wiley Publishing, Inc.

Howell Book House
Published by Wiley Publishing, Inc., Hoboken, New Jersey

Photo Credits: jeanmfogle.com: v, 2, 6, 7, 9, 11, 15, 16, 18, 22, 29, 30 (bottom), 31, 33, 36, 41, 47, 48, 52, 59, 63, 67, 71, 73, 74, 78, 79, 80, 81, 82, 83, 84, 85, 87, 88, 89. ©iStockphoto.com/Hilary O'Connor: 5. ©iStockphoto.com/Giovanni Rinaldi: 10. Lackland Air Force Base: 12. Santa Clara County Fire Department: 17. ©iStockphoto.com/Cheryl Paquin: 20. Working Dogs for Conservation Foundation: 21. Michelle Pelletier: 25. Sheri Wachtstetter: 26, 35. Liz Palika: 30 (top), 40, 44, 55. Lieutenant Governor of Saskatchewan: 34. ©iStockphoto.com/Audrey Stratilatov, 39. Debbie Sparks, 42. Marni Bellavia, 43. Algonquin Hotel, 50. National Park Service photo, 56. ©iStockphoto.com/Jocelyn Lin, 61. Jodi Bratch, 65. ©iStockphoto.com/dra_schwartz, 69. Courtesy of Dude Ranchers' Association & jeff@JAGPhotoInc.com ©2002, 70. ©iStockphoto.com/Bridget McGill, 77. ©iStockphoto.com/Suzanne Tucker, 91.

For general information on our other products and services or to obtain technical support please contact our Customer Care Department within the U.S. at (800) 762-2974, outside the U.S. at (317) 572-3993 or fax (317) 572-4002.

Wiley also publishes its books in a variety of electronic formats. Some content that appears in print may not be available in electronic books. For more information about Wiley products, please visit our web site at www.wiley.com.

Library of Congress Cataloging-in-Publication Data:
Palika, Liz, date.
  Animals at work / Liz Palika, Katherine A. Miller.
     p. cm. — (ASPCA kids)
  Includes index.
  ISBN: 978-0-470-41084-4
  1. Working animals—Juvenile literature. I. Miller, Katherine A. II. Title.

SF172.P35 2009
636.088'6—dc22

2008046335

Printed in China

10 9 8 7 6 5 4 3 2 1

Book design by Erin Zeltner
Book production by Wiley Publishing, Inc. Composition Services

Contents

Chapter 1

Dogs Are Our First and Best Friends   2

People and dogs have been working together for thousands of years. Meet dogs who work on farms and dogs who protect us and keep us safe.

Chapter 2

There's So Much More Dogs Can Do   22

Dogs can help the disabled, cheer up the sad, pull carts, carry things, and more.

Chapter 3

Cats Work, Too   36

From catching mice to greeting hotel guests to saving people's lives, many cats have jobs to do.

Chapter 4

**Hardworking
Horses   52**

Horses work with police officers
and park rangers. They also pull
carts and perform in special
events.

Chapter 5

**Respecting and Caring
for Our Working
Partners   74**

Every working animal needs
and deserves loving care. This
includes plenty of rest, food and
water, medical care, protection,
respect, and a happy,
comfortable retirement.

Resources   92

About the Authors   94

About the ASPCA   95

Index   97

To the degree that we come to understand other organisms we will place greater value on them and on ourselves.

—E.O. Wilson

We cannot do great things on this earth. We can only do small things with great love.

—Mother Teresa

My enjoyment of animals began with Happy, my first dog. She was energetic, loving, fun, and always available for anything—from racing me around the yard to lying quietly by my side while I finished my homework.

But it was the bird feeder at my window that opened up the mystery of it all. From just a few feet away I could watch these alert, colorful creatures nourish themselves while keeping a wary eye on everything around them. I had so many questions about the birds: What did they do all day? Where did they go at night? What happened to them during storms? I thought there ought to be a daily newspaper to report on what had happened the night before in my yard. Who had survived? Who hadn't?

These questions inspired me to observe more and read more about birds. Then I began to learn about other animals—chimpanzees, snakes, and whales—by reading books written by famous authors who spent their lives studying them. Jane Goodall's writing on chimpanzees was the most fascinating to me. But everything I read led to more questions!

My early interest in animals continued to grow. After college, I became involved in creating programs that teach people to care about animals and then became director of an animal shelter in New Jersey. Other positions followed, and eventually I became president of the ASPCA—which stands for the American Society for the Prevention of Cruelty to Animals—the first humane organization in the United States. My childhood curiosity led to a career helping animals, and that enriches my life beyond description.

This past year, the 400-member ASPCA team not only saved the lives of thousands of animals in this country but also enforced the laws designed by our society to protect animals. The mission of the ASPCA from 1866 until the present day is "to provide effective means for the prevention of cruelty to animals." One way the ASPCA does this is through education—through written materials for young people. The books that I read when I was young fed my growing interest in animals. I hope this book will do the same for you.

Edwin J. Sayres
ASPCA President & CEO

1

Dogs Are Our First and Best Friends

People and animals first became friends more than 12,000 years ago. Those animals were wolves, and they started hanging around where the people were because people had food. After a while, people got used to the wolves being nearby and picking up their garbage. The wolves who were not afraid of people came the closest and therefore got the best free meals. Since they were the best fed, they were able to have the most babies. They also taught their cubs not to be afraid of people.

Perhaps someone found a wolf cub and raised him the way we raise puppies today. When that wolf grew up, he decided to stay close to the people and may even have helped them hunt. Eventually a friendship grew, and companionship with people became just as important as food to these animals.

Dogs today are very different from those wolves, but they are still our first animal friends. They are also valuable working partners and do many different jobs.

Herding Farm Animals

Jake is a handsome black and white Border Collie. This breed is best known for its skills in herding sheep, but Jake is different. He herds geese. (Herding means helping to gather and move animals where the farmer wishes them to go.) Geese can be difficult because they are big, and they will peck at and bite dogs. Geese don't have teeth, but they pinch quite hard when they bite. Dogs who herd geese need to be quick to move out of the way when the geese are upset.

Jake's job is to take the geese out of the pen where they spend the night and gently herd them to the grass pasture where they spend their days. Then, in the evening, Jake needs to move them back from the pasture to their pen.

When the geese want to go to their pen, his job is easy. But the geese don't always want to go, and then Jake's job is difficult. He has to run in a circle around all the geese, gathering them together, and then walk behind them. The geese move away from Jake, so when he walks behind them, they move in the direction he wants them to go. Without Jake, the farmer would have to do this all by himself, and the job would be much harder.

Dogs have been herding livestock (farm animals such as cattle, sheep, goats, geese, and ducks) for as long as farmers have kept animals. The dogs may work as Jake does and move the animals from one place to another. They may also gather the animals all together. This is important when the farmer needs to milk the cows or care for the livestock.

When Jake isn't busy herding geese, he plays with the family kids or sleeps in the house. He's a working dog, but he's also a member of the family.

The breeds of dogs used most often today to herd farm animals include Border Collies like Jake, English Shepherds, Australian Shepherds, Australian Cattle Dogs, Shetland Sheepdogs, and Bearded Collies.

The word breed is used to describe dogs (and other animals) who share similar body types and other characteristics. Dogs of a certain breed also have certain working instincts. Australian Cattle Dogs, for example, were bred to help cattle farmers in Australia herd their cattle. Shetland Sheepdogs are small and were bred to herd small sheep on the Shetland Islands in Great Britain.

Protecting Livestock

Predators (animals—wolves, coyotes, and mountain lions, for example—who eat other animals) often try to kill farm animals because they are easier to catch than wild animals such as deer or rabbits. Farmers want to keep predators away from their livestock so they often have dogs known as livestock guardian dogs. These dogs are big—sometimes bigger than the predators—and they protect the livestock from attacks.

Benjamin is a 120-pound Great Pyrenees dog. He is white with cream-color ears, and he has a thick, rough coat. When he was 12 weeks old, the farmer he lives with introduced him to two baby lambs. Ben and the lambs sniffed each other, chased each other back and forth, and then took a nap together. The puppy spent a part of each day with the lambs, getting to know them and beginning to think of them as part of his pack, or family. Dogs are naturally protective of their pack, and Ben was learning that sheep also should be protected.

As he grew up, Ben began spending the night with the flock of sheep. He learned his job by following his mother, Jessie, as she walked around the flock paying attention to the smells and sounds around her, looking for any signs of predators. During the day, Ben and Jessie spend their time with the farmer keeping him company or inside the house with the rest of the family. But each night, Ben is back at work, making sure the sheep are safe from predators.

Barking to Warn Us

Does your dog bark when people knock on your door or ring your doorbell? Most dogs do. One of the first jobs dogs did for people was barking to tell us that other people were approaching.

Dogs who bark when strangers approach are often called watchdogs or alarm dogs. This is because they watch for people and let their families know someone is approaching. For this job, the size of the dog isn't important. Although most people think that large dogs, such as German Shepherds, are the best watchdogs, even small dogs can bark enough to get their family's attention. In fact, many small dogs are more likely to bark than big dogs and so make much better "doorbell dogs"!

Cosmo is a Shih Tzu, a small, fluffy breed of dog. He weighs only 12 pounds, but he has a loud bark. He likes people and is very friendly, but people who come to his family's house may not know that. His barking makes sure they won't enter the house or yard until his human mom, Joanne, gives them permission.

Cosmo is a doorbell dog. He's Joanne's pet. But some dogs work as professional guard dogs protecting property when people aren't around. These dogs are more like employees than pets. The dogs stay in the building or in the business yard, often after it is closed for the day, and bark when anyone approaches. Guard dogs may be trained to bite anyone who breaks in. These dogs are not mean, though. They are valued employees who must be treated with respect, given comfortable quarters and companionship, and rewarded for the hard work that they do.

Finding People Who Are Lost

A dog's nose is much more sensitive than a person's nose. If you sniff a salt shaker, you won't smell anything at all because to us salt has no scent. But dogs can smell salt. In fact, their ability to identify scents is so good that they can even smell salt that has been added to water. This sense of smell makes dogs very good at search-and-rescue work. These dogs search for lost people by using their ability to smell where the people have been. Then the dog's handler (the person who trains the dog and then works with him) calls for help to rescue the lost person.

Michi (pronounced MEE-chee), a big tan and black German Shepherd, is an air-scenting search-and-rescue dog. That means he follows scents that are floating in the air. Scents are created by your body, small pieces of skin (called dander) that fall off, tiny bits of fabric from your clothes, and even the smell of the food you have eaten. All these smells become your own personal scent.

Other breeds, especially Bloodhounds, are trailing or tracking dogs. They follow scents on the ground. When people walk over grass, they drop bits of their personal scent. The grass is also bent and broken and produces its own scents. A tracking dog learns to follow all these smells.

Michi was about 6 months old when he began search-and-rescue training. His handler, Paul, would hold out a piece of clothing that belonged to a person Michi didn't know. When Michi sniffed the clothing, Paul praised him: "Good boy!" Then the owner of the clothing would run a few yards away and hide behind a bush or a tree. Paul told Michi, "Find him!" When Michi followed the person's scent and found him, Paul praised him again: "Yeah! Good boy! Good job!"

As Michi grew up, his practice searches became longer and more difficult. He learned how to follow scents as they moved in the wind or sank to the ground. He learned how to find a scent again when there was a break in the trail.

Paul was learning, too, just as Michi was. He had to know what Michi was doing as he was following the scent. And he needed to know how to help his dog when Michi became confused. Even though Paul couldn't smell the same things that Michi could, he had to learn how weather conditions affect scents and how Michi's nose works. Paul also had to learn how to read a map, a compass, and a GPS (global positioning system, which tells you where you are all the time) so they wouldn't get lost. Paul took a first aid class for people and dogs so that if anyone got hurt on a search, he could help them.

Then, when Michi was 2 years old, he and Paul took a very hard test. They had to search for someone in a forest in Virginia. They passed the test and became a working search-and-rescue team.

On his third official search, Michi worked for three hours trying to find an older man. He had wandered away from his family's home and had become lost in the woods. The man's family said he wasn't feeling well and was confused. During the third hour of searching, Michi's tail began wagging and Paul said, "I think Michi has picked up a scent!"

Sure enough, Michi was sniffing deeply. Soon he made a sharp turn and went up a gully. There, sitting next to a tree, was the lost man. Michi licked his face, and the man put his arms around the German Shepherd, hugging him hard. Paul called for help on his radio, and soon the man was back with his family.

Although German Shepherds and Bloodhounds are often used as search-and-rescue dogs, so are Labrador Retrievers, Golden Retrievers, Bearded Collies, Doberman Pinschers, Australian Shepherds, Bernese Mountain Dogs, and many other athletic breeds with good scenting abilities. There is at least one Pit Bull on record who does search-and-rescue work. Lots of mixed-breed dogs do this work, too.

Water Rescue Dogs

Kody is a big black dog with a thick coat. He also has webbed feet—skin between his toes—like a duck! Kody is a Newfoundland. This breed was developed on the island of Newfoundland in northeastern Canada. These dogs weigh between 130 and 150 pounds and can swim very well, in part due to those webbed feet.

For many years, the people on Newfoundland fished in the rough, cold waters of the Atlantic Ocean. When a boat crashed on the rocks, their dogs would swim out with life rings and ropes and tow the people to shore.

Through the years, many people have been saved by these canine heroes.

Although Kody hasn't had a chance to save any fishermen, he does get to practice his lifesaving skills. He and his human mom, Joan, live in San Diego, California, near the Pacific Ocean. They practice water rescue skills with other Newfoundland dogs and their guardians. One of the people swims out in the water. Then a handler sends her dog with a life ring and rope out to the swimmer. The dog then pulls the person back to shore.

Although no one is drowning—it's just practice—the dogs are very proud of themselves anyway. Joan says, "Dogs enjoy having a job to do. They like being needed, and Kody loves his job of saving people." To help the dogs get better at their job, the Newfoundland Club of America holds water rescue tests where the dogs can show off their skills.

The Dog Scouts of America, an organization that has training programs for dogs and offers dogs and their human parents a chance to earn badges (much like the Girl Scouts and Boy Scouts), has a water safety program. The dogs begin when they are puppies and learn to swim safely. Eventually, they work up to real-life skills. The dogs learn to swim and bring a life ring out to a swimmer in trouble. They also learn to catch an oar that has been dropped in the water and swim it back to the boater who dropped it.

Brave Military Dogs

Experts know that dogs have been helping soldiers for more than 2,000 years. Dogs may have been helping for even longer than that, but we can't know for sure since there aren't many history books available from back then.

One of the first jobs dogs had in the military was to warn the soldiers if people were approaching. Just as your dog barks when someone comes to the door, these army dogs would bark when strangers came too close to camp.

Many military dogs would also use their good scenting abilities to find people, just as search-and-rescue dogs do today. And then, when the army attacked, the dogs would run with the soldiers, barking, growling, and snarling to frighten the enemy.

Today, dogs in the United States Army, Navy, Marine Corps, Air Force, and Coast Guard serve in many different jobs.

- **Sentry dogs.** These dogs work with soldiers, marines, and sailors at sentry gates, where people come into or out of a base. They also work at places where access to a building or area is allowed only to certain people. They growl or bark when people are seen, heard, or smelled.
- **Patrol dogs.** These dogs work alongside military men and women and walk around the base (or ride in a truck) to detect anyone who shouldn't be in that area. They growl or bark when anyone is heard, seen, or smelled.
- **Scout dogs.** These dogs work quietly alongside their military partners, without barking or growling. They are often taught to detect snipers or other enemies by smell, sound, or sight. They alert their handlers that they've found something by sitting or freezing in place, or by changing their body posture.
- **Messenger dogs.** These dogs work for two handlers and run back and forth between them, often over long distances, to deliver

messages. Although cell phones and radios have replaced most messenger dogs, some are still used by the military.

- **Mine detection dogs.** Mines are used to harm the opposing forces' troops. These buried explosives (they're like small bombs) are deadly and kill or hurt many people. Dogs are trained to sniff out buried metals. The dog isn't hurt by the mine, but instead stops, stands still, and points to where the mine is with his nose. Although the military is trying to make machines that can find mines, dogs are still the best at this job. Their abilities have saved thousands of lives.

- **Search dogs.** These military search-and-rescue dogs are taught to find people who may be lost. Some are taught to find certain objects, such as military equipment.

- **Drug detection dogs.** Sometimes the military is called in to help stop people who are trying to bring illegal drugs into the United States. The U.S. Navy and Coast Guard are often involved in these activities, as well as the U.S. Customs Department and the Border Patrol. Dogs who have been taught to find illegal drugs are often called upon to search cars, trucks, boats, and even airplanes to see if any illegal drugs are hidden there.

Dogs are very smart and talented and can be trained to help our military men and women in many different ways. Although a military working dog may have more than one skill—a patrol dog may also have search-and-rescue training, for example—most have one primary job.

In the future, military dogs may be asked to do new jobs that haven't even been thought of yet. Our military men and women also enjoy working with dogs. The waiting list for this job in each branch of the military is usually very long.

There are plans to honor the many dogs who have worked hard in all branches of the military with a national monument. The monument has already been designed. It shows a soldier kneeling with a German Shepherd at his side. A Labrador Retriever sniffs out a trail nearby, and a Doberman Pinscher stands guard. The final location of the National War Dogs Monument has not yet been decided.

The breeds of dogs used by the military depend on the job the dog will be asked to do. If the dog must be watchful, warn of trespassers, and be alert to strangers, the military may use German Shepherds, Belgian Malinois (MAL-in-wah), or other breeds that are naturally protective. If the dog is going to use his scenting abilities and doesn't need to be protective, the military may use Labrador Retrievers, Golden Retrievers, or Beagles.

Hardworking Police Dogs

Just as dogs in the military work alongside soldiers, police dogs work with police officers. A dog is assigned to one officer and works with him or her during their assigned work hours. Then the dog goes home with the police officer when they're off duty. The dog and officer form a close friendship as well as a working relationship.

Police dogs are most often seen riding in a police car with the officer or patrolling busy areas in big cities. If the officer needs help, the dog can come to the officer's assistance. The dog's job may be to chase after the bad guy, biting and then holding him until the officer can put handcuffs on him.

Police work can be dangerous to the officer and his or her dog. Police officers try very hard to keep their dogs safe, often by putting a bulletproof vest on the dog. But this work, called patrol work, is only one of the jobs police dogs perform. Here are some of their other jobs:

- **Crowd control.** The dog and officer can help control crowds of people simply by being nearby and easily seen. People often behave better when they know a police dog is there.
- **Protecting property.** A police dog and officer may be asked to check out property, including homes and businesses, to make sure everything is

okay. Because a dog's senses of smell and hearing are so much better than a person's, the dog can detect problems much sooner.

- ◉ **Finding people.** Just as search-and-rescue dogs have been taught to find people, so have many police dogs.
- ◉ **Finding objects.** Many police dogs are taught to find objects such as guns, bags of money, or other things that criminals might throw away in the hopes they won't be caught by the police. Since the officer may not know what was thrown away, the dog is taught to find an object that is not where it belongs—something that is out of place. A bag of money, for example, doesn't belong in the middle of a grassy field.

- ◉ **Drug detection.** Many police dogs are taught to find illegal drugs in homes, cars, businesses, schools, and other places.
- ◉ **Bomb detection.** Police dogs may also be taught to alert their police officer partner to a bomb or other materials that may explode. The dog doesn't get close to the bomb, but instead stands still and uses his nose to point toward the bomb.

Many police dogs are cross-trained. This means they know how to do more than one job. Many patrol dogs, for example, can also find lost people and lost objects.

During their training, all police dogs learn what is needed for the job they will be doing. Drug detection dogs learn the various smells of illegal drugs, for example, while bomb detection dogs learn to find explosive materials. But all dogs are taught to behave themselves in exciting situations. They learn to ignore gunfire, to be calm in crowds

of people, and to ignore exciting sights such as hot air balloons and sounds such as motorcycles zooming by. Police dogs also learn to ride calmly in cars, trucks, and even helicopters.

Police officers go to school, too. They get to know their dogs and learn to work with them. The police officer has to know how the dog will react when he's excited, worried, or scared. The police officer learns first aid, too, for both people and dogs. If the dog or another police officer gets hurt, the officer can bandage a cut or stop the bleeding.

Police dogs are also great for making friends. Most police dogs are very well trained, and many are very friendly. Police officers may go to schools or public events so that people can get to know the police dog, pet him, and see him perform some of his work. Since these dogs are hard at work, however, always ask a police officer before petting his dog.

German Shepherds and Belgian Malinois are the most commonly used breeds for police work. Police dogs need to be smart, easily trained, and healthy, and they need to be physically strong to do their work. Many, especially patrol dogs, must be powerful enough to catch and hold a bad guy.

What Starts a Fire?

Fires start in many different ways. Sometimes fires begin when lightning strikes the ground and dry grass begins to burn. A fire can start in a home when someone is cooking and the food burns. A candle that is knocked over can start a fire, too.

Sometimes people start fires on purpose. This is called *arson,* and it's against the law. These fires can hurt or kill people and can cause a great deal of damage. It can be difficult for firefighters to determine how a fire began, but it's easier now that some working dogs have been trained to find what started a fire.

Arson-detection dogs are trained to find the kinds of chemicals used to start fires on purpose, including gasoline, lighter fluid, and other materials that burn easily. After a fire has been put out, an arson-detection dog is taken to the place where firefighters think the fire began. If the dog finds the scent of any of these chemicals, he sits with his nose pointing toward them. He is then praised and rewarded for his find. A well-trained arson dog's nose is so sensitive that it can detect even one drop of gasoline.

Deacon is a black Labrador Retriever who works with Mark, a detective with the Oregon State Police Department. Mark and Deacon trained together for this job. Deacon was taught to recognize the chemicals that can start fires. When he finds them, he sits and is given a food treat. The two of them are called in when arson is thought to be the cause of a fire. If Deacon finds several places where fire-starting materials are located, he sits in front of the spot with the strongest smell.

To keep Deacon's skills sharp, he and Mark train often. But when he's at home with Mark, Deacon's a pet and can relax and just be a dog.

The Beagle Brigade

Joyce was in the airport, coming home from a trip to see her sister. She was waiting for her ride home when a small black, tan, and white Beagle wearing a green vest approached her, sniffed her small suitcase, and then walked on past. Joyce had just been checked out by a member of the U.S. Department of Agriculture's (USDA) Beagle Brigade.

The USDA uses Beagles to check for foods and agricultural items that are not allowed into the country. These items are not allowed for many reasons. For example, they may not be of the quality we are used to, or perhaps the items may be carrying insects or parasites that could harm people, livestock, or farms.

Beagles were chosen for this work for several reasons. First, Beagles like to work for food. That makes their training much easier. This love of food also makes it easier to teach the dogs to find food in luggage. Even though the dog isn't given the food that he finds, he is given a treat for finding it.

Beagles also have very good scenting abilities. They can smell traces of foods so small that machinery cannot find it at all. Beagles are small dogs and are able to move through piles of luggage more easily than a larger dog could. The USDA likes to use this breed because most Beagles are healthy and less prone to some of the health problems found in some other dog breeds.

During a Beagle's training, he works with the person who will become his working partner. This way the dog and the person learn to understand each another. The dog is exposed to many different food and plant scents and is taught to find them. When he does, he is taught to sit as close as he can to the food—which might be right next to a suitcase or a package. He is then praised and rewarded for his find.

Other Detection Dogs

The dogs used by the Beagle Brigade are detection dogs. That means they use their scenting abilities to find, or detect, illegal foods and agricultural products. Search-and-rescue dogs can be considered detection dogs, too, because they use their scenting abilities to find people. But dogs can be trained to find other things, as well.

- **Termites.** Termites are insects that eat wood. When termites get into a house, they can eat so much wood that the house can be in danger of collapsing. A person who knows the signs of termite infestation can often find them. But if the termites are hidden in the wood, they may be too difficult for a person to locate. Trained dogs, however, rarely miss because they aren't looking for the termites, they are sniffing for them. They can find termites even when the insects are inside a board or up in an attic.

- **Bedbugs.** These tiny insects live in beds, carpets, curtains, and other dark places where they can hide during the day. They crawl out at night. If they can find a person, they will bite. Many people are allergic to the bite of a bedbug, and each bite turns into a big, itchy red spot. It's hard to see these insects because they run away in the light. Even a flashlight will cause them to hide. But trained dogs can find them quickly by their scent.

- ⊛ **Truffles.** Truffles are a kind of mushroom that grows underground. Many people think truffles are very tasty. Because truffles grow under the dirt, they are hard to find. But dogs have been taught to find them by sniffing out their scent. Although pigs have also been taught to do this job, dogs are preferred because dogs won't eat the truffles they find—sometimes pigs will.

- ⊛ **Mold.** Molds and mildews grow when things are wet for a long time. Houses that have been flooded or have a leaky pipe in the wall often develop mold and mildew. Unfortunately, many molds—especially black mold—can make people very sick. If the mold is inside a wall, the people living in the house may get sick from it without even knowing it's there. Dogs who have been taught to find these molds can do so without endangering themselves, because they alert their handler from a distance to the presence of mold.

Detection dogs can be used to find many things. If a dog can smell something and a dog trainer can teach him to search for that particular scent, then the dog can learn to find it when asked to do so.

Dogs Working for Wildlife

The Working Dogs for Conservation Foundation trains dogs to help people who are working to save threatened or endangered species. This is a new field of work for dogs that is becoming very important. These dogs have been taught to help researchers find and study many different animals, including foxes, black-footed ferrets, bears, turtles, and snakes. Some dogs have even been trained to find certain plants.

Dogs who are able to air scent (follow scents in the air) can learn to follow the scents of specific species. The dogs then work with teams of people who are studying these animals. The dog can help them find the animal's droppings, hair, sleeping places, feeding areas, and, in some cases, the animals themselves. The dog doesn't hunt or catch the animals, but instead leads people to the animals so they can be studied and saved from becoming extinct.

German Shepherds and Labrador Retrievers have been used in this program, but the breed is not as important as the dog's focus on his work. Dogs are chosen who really like to play with toys. If a dog loves his tennis ball, for example, he can be taught to work, and the tennis ball is used as a reward for working.

These talented dogs work in many places around the world. In Africa, dogs have worked with people researching cheetahs and African Hunting Dogs. In Russia, dogs have helped people working to save tigers. In the United States, dogs have located endangered pine snakes in New Jersey and bobcats in California.

There's So Much More Dogs Can Do

In chapter 1, we saw that dogs work with people in many different ways. They help farmers with their livestock and assist police officers. Dogs help military men and women on patrol and do several other important jobs. Dogs even find food hidden in people's luggage. In this chapter, we will continue looking at some of the many ways dogs work with people, helping us and making our lives better.

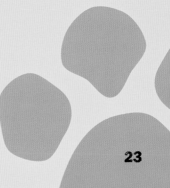

Guiding People Who Cannot See

For thousands of years, dogs have helped people who cannot see. Experts know that in ancient Rome dogs were trained to do this job.

In Germany in the 1800s, Father Johann Klein was the first person to write down exactly how to train a dog to lead a blind person. He also made the first harness for a guide dog that stood up stiffly from the dog's body. This kind of harness made it possible for the person working with the dog to feel the dog's movements and better follow her.

Today, it's not unusual to see dogs assisting people who cannot see. These guide dogs give their people more freedom than they may have had without a dog. The dogs help keep their people safe by watching for obstacles, including curbs and low-hanging tree branches. Guide dogs also learn where their people go regularly and can take them to work, home, and the grocery store.

By law, guide dogs can go anywhere their person goes, including work, the doctor's office, the bank, and a restaurant. Schools that train dogs to be guides for the blind make sure that the dogs they graduate are very well trained and well behaved. Later, their people make sure their training remains sharp. Many guide dog schools require the dogs and their people to come back to the school on a regular schedule to refresh their training.

The guide dog schools try to match each dog with the right person, so that the two can work together well. For example, if a person who walks quickly is paired with a dog who walks slowly, that's not a great match because the dog would slow down the person or the person would try to make the dog speed up. The schools also look at a person's lifestyle. If a person lives in a busy city, the school matches that person with a dog who is able to work despite the distractions of the city's noise and bustle.

German Shepherds were the first dogs used as guide dogs in the United States, but today many different breeds do this work. German Shepherds, Labrador Retrievers, Golden Retrievers, Doberman Pinschers, Australian Shepherds, and even some mixed-breed dogs work as guide dogs.

Assisting People Who Can Use Some Help

Dogs who provide assistance to people are called *service dogs*. Guide dogs who help blind people are service dogs. So are dogs who help people in wheelchairs or need a dog's assistance in other ways.

Service dogs live with their people and spend almost all their time with them. They are hardworking helpers and beloved pets. The bond between a service dog and her person is very close and very special.

Buddy and Hilly

Buddy and his service dog, Hilly, are a team. Wherever Buddy goes, so does Hilly. Hilly is a Labrador Retriever–Golden Retriever mix. She was trained by Canine Companions for Independence in California to assist Buddy in any way she can. Buddy uses a power wheelchair and is active and independent. Hilly makes it easier for him to continue to be that way.

Buddy says, "Hilly can pick up just about anything. She picks up things I have dropped or things that I need. She can do this in the house, picking up the phone, or a pen, or my wallet. Outside, she can bring me the hose, or garden tools, or my gloves. When she picks things up, she will hold them until I ask her to give them to me. And when she gives them to me, she places the things where I can reach them."

He continues, "The other day I was in a store and I tried to swipe my credit card and dropped it. Hilly was trying to pick it up but was having a hard time because it was flat on the floor. The person in line behind me offered to help but I said to give Hilly a chance. She was able to pick it up, and to my surprise, everyone in line behind us began clapping for her. So she not only helped me, but she made the day a little brighter for everyone else, too."

People tend to look at other people who are different. If someone is using crutches, is in a wheelchair, or has a disability, people sometimes stare. Knowing that everyone is looking can make a person feel uncomfortable. Buddy says that when he and Hilly are out together, people tend to watch her, not him, so he feels more comfortable. Service dogs such as Hilly are taught a variety of cues—words or signals asking them to do something. They learn the basic sit, down, and stay cues, and more complicated cues such as opening and closing a refrigerator door. Buddy says that Hilly knows more than 31 cues and is very good at doing them when he asks her to.

Jerry and Rider

Jerry served in the U.S. Army for more than 20 years. He was a good soldier and is proud to have served his country. During his time in the army, he was sent into combat and was wounded.

Jerry says, "I have scars on my leg and arm where I was wounded, but other than a little pain now and then, those have healed up well." However, Jerry has some scars that can't be seen. "Fighting in a war changes you," he says, "and it can be hard to go back to the way you were before you fought in that war." Now when Jerry hears a loud noise, he ducks. He also finds that he gets angry easily. These things happen because of his experiences in combat.

Jerry has been getting help to overcome these emotional problems. In addition, Jerry has a service dog, Rider, who has been trained to help him. Rider is an Australian Shepherd. He senses when Jerry needs his help and responds.

If Jerry is sitting down and starts to feel angry, Rider puts his front feet on either side of Jerry's lap and pushes his head into Jerry's chest. Jerry then hugs the dog, takes deep breaths, and is able to calm himself down. If Jerry is on his feet when Rider senses a problem, Rider steps in front of Jerry, stopping him so he can't walk forward. Jerry then reaches down, touches the dog, talks to Rider, and takes a few breaths to calm himself.

Jerry says, "Rider has probably saved my life. By focusing on him, talking to him, touching him, and through him learning to calm myself, I am enjoying life again."

Working Service Dogs

Hilly and Rider have very different jobs, yet both are service dogs. There are many different kinds of jobs service dogs can do.

- **Hearing assistance.** These dogs are taught to alert hearing-impaired people to specific sounds, such as a baby crying, a teapot whistling, or a telephone ringing. The dogs go everywhere with their people. That way, if a fire alarm goes off somewhere, for example, the dog can alert her person to the danger.
- **Mobility assistance.** Mobility assistance dogs can help people who are in wheelchairs, who walk with crutches or canes, or who

need assistance in other ways to move around safely. Joanne can walk, but her balance isn't very good. Her dog, Luke, a tall and strong German Shepherd, walks by her side. If Joanne loses her balance, Luke braces himself as she grabs his harness and steadies herself.

- ⊛ **Retrieving items.** Service dogs can pick up items that have been dropped or that are needed, such as a telephone or the TV remote. They can also get the newspaper, the mail, or a sweater from the closet. If a dog can pick up an item or drag it, a service dog can be taught to bring it to her person.
- ⊛ **Health alerts.** Dogs pay really close attention to us. Some can even tell us things about our health. Dogs can alert their people to problems such as an oncoming seizure, low blood sugar, or a heart abnormality. When the dog alerts her human partner, the person can then take medication or get help. Some dogs have even been able to detect cancer.
- ⊛ **Emotional or mental health assistance.** These dogs, like Rider, help people who have been hurt or frightened or have other mental health issues. Although emotional or mental health problems are not visible the way physical disabilities may be, the help that service dogs can provide is just as important.

By law, a service dog can go anywhere her person goes. Although dogs are not normally allowed in grocery stores or restaurants, service dogs are. These dogs are well trained so they are not a problem. And their guardians, of course, make sure their dogs are well behaved.

Many different breeds or mixes of breeds work as service dogs. German Shepherds, Labrador Retrievers, Golden Retrievers, Doberman Pinschers, Australian Shepherds, Standard Poodles, and many more can be wonderful working dogs. But smaller dogs can, too. Many hearing assistance dogs and emotional assistance dogs are small dogs. Miniature Poodles, Pomeranians, Yorkshire Terriers, and small mixed breeds serve their people very well.

Providing Love and Affection

Dax, a black, white, and copper Australian Shepherd, carefully placed a front foot on either side of Harry's lap and sniffed his face. Harry bent his head over hers and began to cry. He was a big man, and he pulled the dog to him and released his emotions in heavy sobs. Dax gently swiped her tongue over Harry's face, licking away his tears. After a few moments, Harry let go of the dog, wiped his remaining tears away with the back of his hand, and told those watching, "I had something in my eyes."

Harry had been a resident of Pacific Place in Oceanside, California, for a little more than six months when Dax visited him. Like many people who have Alzheimer's disease, Harry goes through times when his emotions overwhelm him. But when Dax and the other therapy dogs come to visit, those emotions can find a release.

Visiting Therapy Dogs

Therapy dogs and their human partners visit people like Harry who can no longer live in their own homes. Perhaps no one is able to care for them at home, or maybe they need more help than family members can provide.

Chocolate, a miniature Dachshund, and her guardian, Sally, were visiting patients at a hospital. They walked past the room of a woman

who had told them she didn't want any visits. Chocolate, however, decided on this day that she needed to go into the woman's room. The woman had a stroke recently and was very sad. When the dog sat up in front of her wagging her tail furiously, the woman smiled and said, "I don't like dogs, but I like this one!"

Caleb and his partner, Deborah, visit people in a hospice program that provides care for people who are very ill. The program makes it possible for these people to stay at home with their loved ones. Deborah says, "We began visiting Bonnie at her home and would sit out in her backyard. She wasn't able to speak well, but we would watch the birds at her bird feeder, and Caleb would visit with her and then explore her yard. One day when I called, one of her adult children told me she had been unconscious for 24 hours, but to bring Caleb over anyway. Caleb visited with her, providing warmth, affection, and a few licks on the hand. I found out that during her decline, Bonnie had told all of her children about Caleb's visits and how much she had enjoyed them. It warmed my heart to find out Caleb had meant so much to her." So not only did Caleb make Bonnie feel better, but her children were pleased, too, that their mother had a canine friend who visited often.

There is much more that therapy dogs can do.

- ◉ **Paws to read.** Therapy dogs participate in reading programs at schools and libraries. The dog rests quietly next to a child who practices reading out loud to the dog. Dogs seem to really enjoy this. They do not correct pronunciation or other mistakes. Instead, they're simply a warm, affectionate audience.
- ◉ **Ask before petting.** Many therapy dogs visit day-care centers and schools to help kids learn how to prevent dog bites. Kids can learn how to approach dogs safely and how to ask for permission to pet a dog. They also learn what to do if they are confronted by a dog they do not know and who is not on a leash.
- ◉ **Aid in healing.** Some visiting therapy dogs work with people who are caring for patients. They encourage the patients to do the

things they need to do to get better. For example, someone who is supposed to exercise an arm may be more willing to do her exercises by brushing a dog or throwing a ball for the dog. People may be more willing to try out a walker or a wheelchair if the dog goes for a walk with them.

⊛ **Motivation to try.** Experts have found that dogs can be great motivators. People who can't speak are more willing to try to talk if a dog is present. A patient who can't move an arm may be more willing to try if they can pet a dog. People are also more willing to talk with other people if a dog is cuddled close.

Experts who have studied therapy dogs have found that these friendly, affectionate dogs can provide many benefits to people. People being visited by a dog feel cared for and loved. The dog provides affection, which is important to everyone. People also need to touch other warm living things, and a dog is wonderful to hug.

Therapy dogs can be any breed and any size. Sasha is a Rottweiler who weighs 120 pounds, while Mitzi is a Maltese who weighs only 3 pounds. Both are wonderful therapy dogs. Any breed, or mix of breeds, can make a good therapy dog. Therapy dogs just need to be very friendly, social with people, and well trained.

There are several groups, including the Delta Society and Therapy Dogs International, that have testing programs to ensure therapy dogs are well trained, safe, and able to do the work. The dogs are tested on their obedience skills—sit, down, stay, walk nicely, and more—as well as their behavior around people. The dogs cannot jump on people, paw, or scratch, and they must be calm around walkers, wheelchairs, and other equipment they might encounter on a visit.

Pulling Sleds and Wagons

Many years ago animals helped people get from one place to another. They also carried things on their backs or pulled wagons or sleds. Although horses, donkeys, and mules were more commonly used for getting around (read more about them in chapter 4), dogs were also a great help to many people.

Draft Dogs

Horses and other large animals are expensive to keep. Not everyone could afford their food and care. But in the days when animals were used to pull and carry, most people could feed a dog because the dog ate what her people ate. Many people who couldn't keep a horse but needed help built small wagons. They kept large dogs to pull those wagons. Dogs who were used to pull wagons were (and still are) called *draft dogs,* just as horses used to pull wagons are called *draft horses.*

Some dog breeds still pull wagons and carts today, both to assist their people and in competitive sports. A dog who is well trained and is strong and muscular can help in many ways by pulling a wagon. If the person has a big bag of potting soil, for example, the dog can pull the wagon with the potting soil to the backyard. Trash cans can be loaded into a wagon, and the dog can pull it to the curb.

Bernese Mountain Dogs were once used on dairy farms in Switzerland to pull carts full of milk. The Bernese Mountain Dog Club of America celebrates the breed's history as a working companion by hosting competitions for dogs who know how to pull a wagon. Other breeds, including Newfoundlands, Rottweilers, Saint Bernards, and Greater Swiss Mountain Dogs, also compete in wagon-pulling competitions, called *carting.*

Many dog training clubs have carting classes so that dogs and their people can learn how to participate in this sport safely. The well-trained dogs can often be seen in holiday parades, pulling decorated wagons carrying local children.

Sled Dogs

Dogs have been used to pull sleds in the snow for hundreds of years. The native peoples of far northern Canada and Alaska used sled dogs to haul food home from the hunt. The dogs also helped people travel in the winter when the snow was too deep to walk in easily. In Siberia, the native people developed the breed of dogs now known as Siberian Huskies. These dogs helped herd reindeer and were also used to pull sleds.

In the early 1900s, many people were unaware of the value of sled dogs. But then in 1925, people in Nome, Alaska, began dying of an outbreak of diphtheria, a contagious disease. The medicine to help the town was available in Anchorage, but the weather was too bad for an airplane to fly it in. So teams of sled dogs were gathered. In five and a half days, the sled dog teams and their drivers, called *mushers*, carried the medication 674 miles to Nome. By doing so, they saved many people's lives.

Today, people also ski behind their sled dogs. This fun sport is called *skijoring*. People also let a sled dog pull a child on a sled for fun. Some people compete in official sled dog races, usually because these dogs absolutely love to run and pull on a cold winter's day. Breeds developed in the cold north, such as Siberian Huskies, Alaskan Malamutes, and Samoyeds, sometimes work as sled dogs. So do many mixes of the northern breeds.

Entertaining Us All

People are fascinated by a well-trained dog. Watching a guide dog or a service dog work makes us sigh with pride that a dog can be so talented and devoted. Watching a therapy dog snuggle up to someone's grandmother brings tears to our eyes. Listening to a child read to a dog in the library fills us with joy.

This fascination with dogs who help us has made dogs very popular in the entertainment industry. We see dogs in movies, television shows, and commercials. Dogs are pictured in magazines, and even our favorite characters in books are sometimes dogs. Dogs are in every part of our lives.

Kate has a Cocker Spaniel–Poodle mix named Walter. Walter is a bright, active dog. If he's not kept busy, he tends to get into mischief. Kate began teaching Walter tricks just to keep his training fresh and exciting, and to keep him out of trouble. She soon found that Walter was very good at learning tricks. He could bow to an audience, sit up and beg, weave through her legs as she walked, and play dead. Within a couple of years after beginning his lessons, Walter knew more than a hundred different tricks.

One day, when Kate went to a pet fair, she saw that a company that finds trained dogs for movies, television shows, and commercials was looking for new faces. She signed up for an audition. When they arrived, the person interviewing Kate asked what Walter could do. When Kate began listing his tricks, the interviewer was very impressed!

Walter's photograph has already been published in several books, and he's been mentioned in magazine articles. Kate says, "I would love to see Walter on TV or in a movie. I would burst with pride. But realistically, I know that a small, black, fuzzy dog is hard to photograph." That's because black dogs have black eyes and black noses, so their features don't stand out very well in photos. But someday, if you see a small, black, fuzzy Cocker Spaniel–Poodle mix on television or in a movie, wave and say, "Hi!" It may just be Walter, the trick dog.

Cats Work, Too

People and cats have a long, interesting history together. About 10,000 years ago, people began planting gardens rather than roaming the landscape to collect wild plants to eat. With gardens to supply many of their foods, people settled down and stopped moving their homes. Because they could grow more food than they could eat, they began storing food for the future. Animals such as mice and rats moved in to eat those foods. Wild cats, who naturally hunt mice and rats, followed.

As cats and people lived closer together, people began to see the advantage of having cats in their lives. Cats did (and still do) hunt the mice and rats that spoil stored foods. Then someone petted a purring cat and found out how enjoyable cats can be. A relationship was born.

As cats became more important in people's lives, the relationship changed. In the beginning, the cat was simply a hunter who caught rodents. But in ancient Egypt, the cat was looked upon as a sacred animal—something to be treasured. The huge statue of the sphinx in Egypt has the head of a human and the body of a lion. The Egyptians had a goddess who looked like a cat, too. They called her Bastet.

Today, cats are well-loved pets and companions who live in our homes and share our beds. Although cats don't work for people the same way dogs and horses do, cats are workers in their own unique ways.

Pest Control Today

Rats and mice are still with us today, eating our food and causing problems. They spread diseases to people and to our domesticated animal friends. In addition, rats and mice can carry parasites such as fleas, ticks, and internal worms.

Cats, meanwhile, are natural predators, and rodents are their prey. At one time or another, many cat people have found a dead mouse that the cat caught. If there are no mice around, cats will hunt and kill bugs. Cats love to hunt, and they also like to show us what they have caught—even if we don't want to see it!

Cats in Businesses

Many businesses take advantage of the cat's amazing hunting abilities by using them to help control rodents. In some areas of New York City, for example, rats are a huge problem. They get into buildings, chew holes in walls, chew wires, and eat the food in grocery stores and kitchens. They leave urine and feces wherever they go. The rats scare people and create a serious health hazard.

Andre has a small shop in New York City, and he no longer has a rodent problem. The solution was a small black and white cat named Cookie. She has been in his shop for six years. Cookie has her own bed near the cash register, and customers pet her as they pay for their purchases. Andre says, "No one has ever complained about Cookie being here. In fact, if she's not on the counter, they ask for her. And if she weren't here, the rats would be back right away."

Of course, New York City is not the only place rats and mice live. So cats are needed everywhere. Two cats live at an antique shop in Julian, California. The cats weren't planned additions. They appeared on the store's front step as kittens. The store owners weren't planning to keep them in the store. But they had a mouse problem, and they saw that the mice began to disappear when the kittens moved in. The brother and sister tiger-striped cats, Sam and Tabby, are now 10 years old, and they're favorites with the customers. Sam likes to sit in the middle of an aisle and meow until people stop to pet him. Tabby jumps up on furniture so that she is right at hand level and easier to pet.

Although Cookie, Tabby, Sam, and other cats like them are in the business of rodent control, they are still treasured pets. They don't have to rely on the mice or rats they catch for their food. Instead, they get good cat food to eat, go to the veterinarian when needed, and are an important part of the shop owners' (and employees') lives. And the customers' lives, too!

Many times, mice and rats disappear from a business or home not just because the cat catches them but also because the rodents smell the scent of the cat and stay away.

Cats in the Barn

Katy has several horses. She keeps feed for the horses in a shed, but says, "No matter how I fix up the shed, the mice and rats still find a way in. They get into the horses' feed and grain, eat some, and spoil more. So I have cats to help me keep the rodents away."

Katy's cats are well fed, well groomed, and spayed or neutered, so they can't have kittens. (A spayed or neutered cat is less likely to roam and is happier to stay at home. It's also important for a cat to be spayed or neutered because there are far too many kittens looking for homes than there are homes available for them.) When Katy's cats are not hunting mice and rats in the horse shed, they are in the house. One of them, Macho, is a huge longhaired orange and white cat with a sweet, gentle personality. Macho is very dignified and doesn't ask for petting. But when he is petted, he will lie down so that his tummy can be rubbed.

Another of Katy's cats, Lady, is a beautiful, brightly colored calico shorthaired cat. (*Calico* refers to Lady's color pattern, which is white with bright orange and black markings.) Lady is a talker. All the guests who come to see the horses immediately learn that she is the farm greeter. She meows as she winds between legs until people reach down to pet her. People have to step carefully so they don't trip over Lady. And if someone picks her up, she purrs so loudly that she vibrates all over.

Although Katy's cats help her by hunting for mice and rats in the shed, the most important thing is that they are her pets and companions.

Cats, Books, and Libraries Go Together

Kittens are very playful and, like all young animals, can get into a lot of trouble. But adult cats tend to spend more time quietly enjoying the world around them. This can make them perfect working animals in libraries, where everyone must keep their voices down.

Cats Encourage Reading

Jason loves to read now, but he didn't always. The blond 10-year-old says, "My mom would bring me to the library, but I just liked to look at the pictures. I didn't like to read." His mom says, "One day when Jason was sitting at the table in the library flipping through the pages of a book, Samantha the cat came up and settled down next to his book. Jason began petting her and talking to her. The librarian told him, 'Why don't you read to Samantha? She likes that.' Jason read to the cat for an hour."

Jason's mom says that ever since then, Jason has looked for Samantha. If she isn't with another kid, he reads to her. He really loves to read now, even when he's not reading to Samantha.

Library Cats Are Everywhere

The Spencer Public Library in Spencer, Iowa, had a library cat named Dewey. (Dewey was named for the Dewey Decimal System, the system that librarians use to organize all the books in the library.) He was abandoned in the library book drop as a half-frozen kitten on a bitterly cold January day. Dewey lived to age 19 and was so famous that he got fan mail from people all over the world. A Japanese television crew even went to Iowa to film him.

In Mystic, Connecticut, the library cat is Emily. She's named after the famous authors Emily Brontë and Emily Dickinson. She enjoys riding on the revolving bookcase that introduces new books, and she encourages people to pet her by lying on her back with all four paws in the air.

Funi is a deep reddish-orange tabby cat who lives in the National Library of Iceland. Inside the library, Funi has his own cat tree where he can climb, groom his claws, and take a catnap.

Books is a gray and black tabby cat with a white muzzle, white chest, and four white feet. Books lives in the Horsham College Library in Australia.

All over the world, people have found that a friendly cat can be a wonderful addition to a library. Cats in libraries are welcoming and calming. People enjoy having a warm cat in their lap as they read a book. Kids find they enjoy reading to a cat—and the cat never points out mistakes.

Therapy Cats Give Love

Therapy dogs tend to get a lot of attention. Dogs give sloppy wet kisses and wag their tails all the time. But some people would prefer to snuggle with a warm, purring cat. Luckily for them, cats can be therapy pets, too.

A Cat Named Flea

Flea is a brown, black, and tan striped tabby cat who really enjoys cuddling with people. He got his name because as a kitten, when he was adopted from the local shelter, he was tiny, brown, and jumped around like a bug! When he grew up, every time visitors came to his family's house, Flea would jump in the guests' laps. He'd purr and nudge their hands until they petted him.

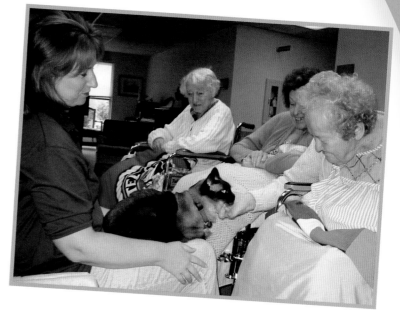

His human parent, Paul, did visiting therapy work with his dog, so he asked about bringing Flea along, too. Therapy pets—dogs, cats, horses, and other animals—visit people to share love and affection. They go to nursing homes, schools, libraries, hospitals, and even day-care centers for very young children.

Before Flea could begin visiting people, he had to visit the veterinarian to make sure he was healthy. And he had to learn to walk nicely on a halter. When the person in charge of the therapy visits saw that Flea was also kind, calm, and well behaved, Flea was given the okay to begin.

Flea's first visit was to a home for older people who need help caring for themselves. He walked in the door with several dogs. He walked right up to a gentleman in a wheelchair, jumped in the man's lap, and nudged his hand until the man started petting him. As he was stroking Flea's head, the man said "This cat's quite the character, huh? Real bashful, he is." (He really meant Flea wasn't bashful at all!)

Flea has been visiting people for 10 years now. Two or three times a month, he shares warmth and affection with older men and women who may be lonely or not feeling well. Or maybe they miss the pets they shared their lives with years ago. Flea always manages to cheer them up.

Laser Gives Hugs

Laser, a blue-eyed Siamese, is another therapy cat. In fact, Laser was named the ASPCA Cat of the Year for 2006 because of his nine years of work as a visiting therapy cat.

Laser and his human mom, Nancy, have been visiting kids and adults in hospitals. When Laser greets someone in the hospital, he wraps his paws around their neck to give them a hug. Sometimes people are startled to get a hug from a cat, but they always enjoy both the hug and Laser.

Big Bubba Is Calm

Bubba, a big brown and black tabby cat, was a huge part of a very special therapy visit. A teenage girl named Michelle was hurt in an accident and was not responding to anyone, not even her mother. Therapy dogs came in to see her, but even during their visits, Michelle didn't move or open her eyes.

Michelle's mother said that Michelle liked cats, so Nicole brought her therapy cat, Bubba, to Michelle's hospital room. When Nicole placed Bubba on Michelle's bed, the cat walked over to Michelle, tucked himself under her arm, and began to purr. Nicole says, "He was purring so hard that all of us in the room could hear him."

Within moments Michelle opened her eyes, looked at Bubba, and began humming under her breath. Bubba rolled on his back, showing his white tummy, and Michele tried to move her arms so she could pet him. Her mother placed Michelle's hand on Bubba, and Michele was able to move by herself. It was the first time she had been able to do that since her accident.

Nicole says, "Everyone in the room was so excited, we were crying. But at the same time, we didn't want to make a sound or move because we didn't want to change this magic moment." Nicole and Bubba continued to visit Michelle twice a week until Michelle was well enough to go home. Once she was home, she asked her mom if she could have a cat of her own. They adopted a cat from a local shelter.

Cats Can Be Heroes, Too

When people think of animal heroes, they usually think of dogs first and then maybe horses. But cats can be heroes, too. Cats can warn people about danger and even go to get help. Although cats tend to be independent, people who love cats know that cats are devoted to their people.

Wonderful Winnie

Winnie, a 14-year-old shorthaired cat, was named the ASPCA Cat of the Year for 2007 because she saved her family's lives. Winnie woke up her person, Cathy, in the middle of the night, clawing, scratching, and meowing. The house was filling up with poisonous fumes that could have killed the entire family in their sleep, and Winnie smelled them. Once she was awake, Cathy called 911, and the paramedics rescued the family and Winnie. Everyone is fine.

Cathy had found Winnie when she was just a few days old, abandoned at a neighboring farm. She nursed the kitten with an eyedropper, saving her life. Years later, Winnie saved her family's lives. That's a hero!

Brave Hank

Hank, a silver, brown, and black tabby cat, was outside with his family (a cat should never be outside alone!) when a black bear wandered into their backyard in rural North Carolina. The bear was apparently looking for berries to eat, but Hank decided the bear was a danger to the family's three children. With his fur standing on end to make him look bigger, Hank charged the bear, meowing loudly and hissing, until the bear climbed a tree.

Hank's human parent, Charles, says, "We had a hard time getting Hank to come inside so the bear could leave. I finally had to pick him up and carry him inside and then lock the door because he kept trying to push the door open."

We Love Watching Cats

Have you ever watched a cat run and jump? Cats are strong, graceful, and athletic. People enjoy watching cats, so they have been featured in television shows, commercials, and movies. Have you seen the beautiful white longhaired Persian cat in cat food commercials? You may not remember the name of the cat food, but you certainly remember that pretty cat eating from a fancy dish.

It takes a special cat to be able to perform in TV shows, movies, and commercials. The cat needs to be calm and able to handle all the sights, sounds, and smells of the area where the filming takes place. Most cats are happiest at home, but cats who star in TV shows, movies, or commercials need to be happy away from home, too.

Although many people seem to think cats can't be trained, that's not true. With feline-friendly training techniques, every cat can be a star, even if it's just in your living room. Here are some suggestions for training all types of cats:

- Cats need to meet a variety of people, not just those who live with the cat. When cats know only people at home, they can become frightened when they meet strangers. A scared cat may bite, scratch, and try to escape. If a frightened cat is outside and runs away, he could be lost forever. Introductions to other people need to be happy and friendly, and they are best done when the cat is young.

- Cats also need to be comfortable with other animals. Again, these introductions need to be very happy and positive, and they are best done when the cat is young. Never let the other animal frighten the cat.
- The cat should be comfortable riding in the car in her carrier.
- The cat needs to be comfortable wearing a harness and walking on a leash.
- The training should be very positive, meaning never yell at the cat, hit him, jerk his leash, or do anything to punish him. Instead, use treats that the cat likes (such as tiny bits of chicken or tuna) to help him understand what is being asked of him. If you give him a treat every time he does the right thing, he'll quickly figure out what he needs to do to get more treats. The treats are also rewards for when the cat succeeds at his tasks.

One-of-a-Kind Working Cats

Sometimes cats create their own jobs. Many cats are very social; they enjoy being with people or with other animals. Sometimes, a cat wanders into a place and meets some friendly people who pet him or offer food. This makes the cat happy, especially if he was alone and hungry. A cat in this situation often chooses to stay. These formerly stray cats become loved and cherished indoor pets.

Biscuit

Biscuit, a cream, yellow, and orange striped tabby cat, was the resident cat at a veterinary hospital in San Clemente, California, for many years, beginning in the mid-1970s. No one quite remembers how Biscuit arrived. The receptionist thought the cat just wandered in the front door and decided not to leave. One of the veterinary technicians thought he came in with a client who never came back to pick him up. But how he arrived didn't seem to matter. Although veterinarians and staff members came and went, Biscuit stayed.

The friendly cat spent a lot of time on the front counter. He would greet everyone who came into the clinic—even dogs and their people. If a dog was rowdy and jumping up on the counter, Biscuit would pop the dog on the nose with a front paw, although he never used his claws. If a client brought in a bird, Biscuit would watch carefully but never tried to hunt or catch the bird.

In emergencies where another cat needed a blood transfusion, Biscuit would serve as the donor, allowing the veterinarian to put a needle in the vein of his front leg and take a small amount of blood—just enough to help the injured cat but not enough to hurt Biscuit. After being a blood donor, Biscuit always got a very special meal as a reward.

No one knew how old Biscuit was because he was an adult cat when he moved in. But when he got older and his joints were stiff, the receptionist at the clinic, Dorothy, said she would take Biscuit home so he could retire in peace and quiet. But even after giving him time to adjust, Biscuit wasn't happy. Apparently he enjoyed all the attention the clients gave him, so he came back to the clinic. When he passed away of old age, a small plaque was put on the counter where his bed always was, saying simply, "Biscuit. A Very Good Cat."

The Hotel Cat

The Algonquin Hotel in New York City is an elegant hotel with a fancy lobby. There are sofas with pillows where guests who have been walking around the city all day can relax, and chairs are grouped together so that business people can talk. But one piece of furniture is not like the others. Just to one side of the entrance door of the lobby is a small sofa that's reserved for the resident cat.

The hotel has had a resident cat since the 1930s. At that time, the general manager, Frank Case, took in a wet and unhappy cat who was looking for shelter. Case named him Rusty. Rusty, later named Hamlet, was so popular with the hotel guests that when he died, the Algonquin Hotel got another cat. They've had cats ever since.

Today's resident cat is a female named Matilda. She is a Ragdoll cat, a large, longhaired breed, and she enjoys spending time on her miniature sofa in the lobby. She also mingles with guests. In November 2006, Matilda was named the Cat of the Year at the Westchester Cat Show in White Plains, New York.

Bob

Bob, a brown and black tabby cat with short hair, has his own blog. (A blog is like a diary online that other people can read.) Bob is the resident cat at the Inn at the Moors in Provincetown, Massachusetts. In his blog, Bob says he's in charge of tourism, bringing in people to stay at the inn and keeping the guests happy.

In his July 2008 blog, Bob wrote that he enjoys summer evenings, hot dogs on the grill, and all the people at the inn. He also said the blueberries will be ripe soon.

What Bob doesn't say, however, is how he figured out how to use the computer. Perhaps the owner of the inn helps him and just lets Bob take all the credit.

Cats in the Workplace

Cats are in many workplaces today. Although some cats control rodents, many cats come to work just to keep people company, make people laugh, and help relieve the stress of a busy day. Sid Vicious (the cat, not the punk rock star) was adopted from an Indiana shelter and soon became a full-time employee at Halstead Architects. Natural Stone Specialist in Carmel, Indiana, has a resident cat, Lily, as well as a dog and three birds.

As I write this book, an orange and white cat with medium-long hair is lying to my left. When I reach for the mouse to my computer, she gently pats my hand as if to say, "Hey! I catch all the mice here!" Squash and her sister, Pumpkin, keep me company every day while I write. They take turns on the desk or on the windowsill just to the right of my computer. When I get up from the computer desk, they do, too, and follow me around the house. They are great company.

Hardworking Horses

Horses and people have worked together for thousands of years. People who have studied this relationship think horses were first used for riding and then for carrying heavy loads. Later, when people understood how strong horses are, they began to use horses to pull farm tools, wagons, and sleds. Before we had cars and trucks, horses were the main way people traveled long distances. For thousands of years, horses were an important part of everyday life.

Friendship and Riding

Although horses work for people, they can still be great friends. In fact, most people who have a horse as a working partner consider their horse to be a very good companion.

Out on the Trail

Audrey, who has two horses, says, "Horses are different from dogs and cats because they live outside instead of in your house. That means you don't get to cuddle up in bed with them or sit on the couch with them watching TV. But you can still have a close friendship with your horse."

She says, "Some horses come when you call them, and they 'talk' to you. My horse Milagro, who is a Spanish Mustang, calls to me in a happy tone of voice whenever he sees me. He comes up to the edge of his paddock (a small fenced-in field) and sticks his head out, waiting for a scratch on the forehead or a kiss on the muzzle."

Milagro is light brown and has a black mane, tail, and legs—a color combination called *dun.* Audrey says, "Both my horses, Milagro and Red, a chestnut-colored Quarter Horse, are very good to ride. As soon as you get on them, they know their jobs. My husband, Randy, and I use them for trail riding. They take us out on the trail for hours at a time. They not only provide us with a ride, but they also give us companionship."

A Dream Come True

Petra keeps her horse, Raz (short for Razzle Dazzle), in a corral in her side yard. She says, "As a young girl I always dreamed of having a horse. Now, many years later, I've been able to make my dream come true. Raz, a black Morgan

Horse with a white blaze on his face, is a very good friend. He loves it when I use my long fingernails and scratch him. He will wiggle his lips and make funny faces when I scratch certain spots."

Petra adds, "Raz is a young horse, just 3 years old, and, like all kids, he likes to play. He has a big orange traffic cone that he likes to pick up in his teeth. He'll swing his head and send the traffic cone flying. Then he'll go get it and do it again. He's very funny."

When Raz grows up, he will be a riding horse for Petra, just as Audrey's horses are for her and her husband. Although their horses are pets, friends, and companions, they also work hard by carrying people on their backs, minding their manners, and keeping their riders safe.

A Growing Friendship

Cayla is 15 years old. She has many friends at school, but one of her best friends is a Morgan Horse named Charm. At first Cayla was a little bit afraid of horses. One had kicked her, so she was very aware of how hard a horse's hooves are. Cayla says, "Horses have teeth at one end and hard hooves at the other end." Plus, horses are really big!

But as Cayla got to know Charm, she found out that Charm, who is 10 years old, is a well-mannered lady. She is gentle and likes to follow Cayla all over. And when Cayla rides her, Charm takes good care of Cayla.

Charm is also a good listener. While Charm is eating, Cayla sits nearby and talks to her horse. Charm listens but never offers advice. Everyone needs someone to talk to.

Park Patrol

Many cities, counties, and states have large parks where people go to enjoy the outdoors. They may go for a hike in the woods, relax on the green grass of a lawn, or play games. When people work inside all day, getting outside can be very enjoyable. Horses and their riders who patrol these large parks help make sure everyone is safe and no one gets lost.

A Park Patrol Horse

Ari watches the sun come up, stretches, shakes his long mane, and nickers softly. His human partner, Terry, is in the house but hears him and calls out, "Good morning, Ari! How are you?" Ari, whose name means *eagle* in the Icelandic language, is a 20-year-old black and white pinto Icelandic Horse. Since Terry is now awake, Ari knows that breakfast will be coming soon, so he watches the house.

As she feeds him his breakfast, Terry talks to Ari and strokes his neck. Ari has been her friend for ten years, and she enjoys his company. After she puts his food out, she leaves him alone to eat and goes inside to have her own breakfast.

After breakfast, Ari gets a drink and strolls around his corral in Terry's backyard. He watches a bird flying overhead and sniffs the breeze. He's waiting patiently—he knows that Terry will be coming back outside soon to brush him, comb out his mane and tail, check his feet, and then load him in the trailer. Today is a work day, and Ari enjoys the job he and Terry do.

Terry says, "Ari and I are mounted patrol rangers for the city of Poway, in California. There are more than a hundred miles of trails around Lake Poway, and we make sure people don't get lost. We also check to see that people have enough water, and we help them if they need help. We also make sure the trails are safe, that the bridges are sound, and that trees or branches haven't blown down."

In the bags attached to his saddle, Ari carries extra water, clippers for branches, an emergency first aid kit, a cell phone, and other supplies that might be needed. Ari and Terry patrol the park once a week, so Ari gets plenty of time to relax between patrols.

Sometimes Ari and Terry are able to help people. Terry says, "One day a woman fell off her horse and was hurt. She was on the ground and her horse ran off. I called 911 and went off after her horse while someone else stayed with the woman. Ari and I found her horse about half a mile away. When help came for the woman, we told her that her horse would be safe until she could get him, and we took the horse home with us."

Park Patrol Horses Are Special

Not every horse can do this job. Patrol horses must be calm in an emergency and must be steady around strange noises and objects, including strollers, bikes, balloons, fire engines, and motorcycles. Terry says, "Ari loves patrols. He enjoys having kids pet him and he likes to watch the wildlife we see, including deer, foxes, bobcats, and even coyotes."

Terry says, "Having patrol horses like Ari on duty make people feel safer when they are out hiking. Plus, Ari can get me to help faster than I could ever walk."

Many other parks have horse patrols, too. New York City has mounted patrols in several parks, including the huge and famous Central Park, Clove Lakes Park, and Van Cortlandt Park. To be a member of the park patrol, both horses and riders must go through a lot of training. The people need to be good riders, know how to use portable radios, and know the rules that apply to the parks. The horses need to be very well trained and safe around all kinds of sights and sounds, including people, dogs, vehicles, and anything else they might come across in the parks.

Providing Therapy for People

Horses can be good for people. Not only are horses excellent listeners, but touching a warm, breathing, friendly animal is good for us. We feel better when we stroke, pet, and brush a horse. We laugh when the horse does something silly, and that's good for us, too. But horses can do even more than that.

Riding Programs Make People Feel Better

Experts have discovered many benefits to riding horses. Because horses walk smoothly and with a rocking motion, riders gain balance, build muscles, and find they are able to move more easily. And as people ride a horse more, they feel better about themselves and are happier.

The Helen Woodward Animal Center in San Diego, California, has an active horse therapy program. There's a staff of ten who are trained to assist people with a variety of disabilities. The people who come to ride their calm, gentle horses range in age from 4-year-old children to 70-year-old senior citizens. The riders learn better balance and posture, gain better hand-eye coordination (how well they react to what they see), and can even improve their short-term memory.

The horses seem to know when they are helping someone. Lisa, the riding supervisor, says, "When Questa, a horse who has been in our program for nine years, has an able-bodied rider, she's not very cooperative and sometimes acts up. But when her rider is disabled, she's all work, serious, and a model employee."

One of the organizations that helps make sure horses used in riding programs are safe is the North American Riding for the Handicapped Association. This group helps train the people who will be working with the horses, helps set up lesson plans, and visits the stables where riding will be taking place. All of this is to make sure that both people and horses will benefit from these programs.

Visiting Therapy Horses

Some horses are too small to ride, but even these small horses can help people. Scooter is a brown and white Miniature Horse who is a visiting therapy horse. (Miniature Horses are very small, often no taller than a big dog, although they weigh more than a dog.) Scooter joined Nicole's family when he was rescued from a bad situation. Nicole, who was recovering from a serious accident, found Scooter to be calm, friendly, and loving. His love and affection helped her heal from her injuries.

When she was better, she began taking Scooter to a school for therapy visits with children who needed help. She says, "The children loved him, of course, and he was always very calm with them. But the teachers always wanted to pet him, too, and would greet him on every visit." Today, Scooter still visits children. He also visits homes for older people, especially those who need some special love.

The Foundation for Pet-Provided Therapy is one of several organizations that evaluate horses, as well as dogs, cats, rabbits, and other pet animals, for visiting therapy work. Horses must be well trained, which includes walking on a lead rope and standing still while being petted. The horses cannot do anything that would hurt people, so biting and kicking are not allowed. The horses are not required to be housetrained because most visits occur outside of a building. But a housetrained horse is wonderful because then the horse can visit people who may not be mobile enough to come outside to see her.

Police Horses

Many police departments, sheriffs' departments, and private security companies use horses in their work. Although many horses have been replaced by off-road motorcycles, four-wheeled off-road vehicles, and bicycles, horses can still perform a vital service for both the police and the people the police are protecting.

Police Horses Have Many Jobs

Police officers on horses can serve many purposes. In cities, horses can patrol in places where cars can't, such as crowded streets and sidewalks. On horseback, the police officers are above the crowd and can see what's going on. The police officers can enforce the law, watch to make sure everyone is okay, and prevent problems. People are also less likely to argue with a police officer on horseback than a police officer standing on the ground.

Police horses can work with the officers in other ways, too.

- In rural areas and even in cities, a horse can go places where a car can't.
- A horse causes less damage to the ground than a car or an off-road motorcycle does.
- Police horses walk in parades, usually in a group with other horses or in a color guard. Mounted color guards are four horses who walk side by side. The riders carry flags (called the "colors"), usually the American flag, the state flag, and often the flags of the police department. The color guard often leads the parade or begins special events.
- Police horses help look for bad guys and criminal suspects who may be trying to escape from the police.

- Because horses walk faster than people can, police horses enable the officers to patrol an area more quickly.

- Police departments have also found that police horses create goodwill. People like horses. Kids (and adults) like to pet the horses and many want to have their picture taken standing next to the horses.

- Police horses are also used in search-and-rescue work. Because a mounted officer has better visibility and the horse can walk faster than a person can, a horse can be a big help when looking for a lost person. The officer learns to pay attention to his or her horse because the horse may hear or see something the officer doesn't. That might just be the person they are looking for.

Polite and Well Trained

Police horses must be very well trained so that they remain safe. These are some of the skills that police horses must have.

- Be able to be led by a person on the ground at a walk or a trot.

- Stand quietly for grooming, veterinary care, and the farrier (a person who takes care of the horse's feet and shoes).

- Stand quietly to have the saddle and bridle (riding equipment) put on.

- Stand still for one minute with a rider in the saddle.

- With a rider in the saddle, be able to walk over many different surfaces, including a tarp on the ground, grass, gravel, dirt, sand, concrete, and asphalt, and through water.

- With a rider in the saddle, be able to step over obstacles, such as logs on the ground and curbs.
- With a rider in the saddle, be safe around different sights and sounds, including a flapping raincoat and a loud police whistle.
- With a rider in the saddle, be able to back up and step sideways to the left and to the right.

During training, the horses and riders are exposed to many different situations. This makes sure they and the people around them will be safe once the horse is out on the street working. Some of the different things the horses see include a six-foot beach ball that rolls on the ground. The horses learn to push it, move out of its way, and understand that it isn't dangerous. The horses and riders also walk through strips of hanging plastic, like strips of a shower curtain, that might initially be scary—but that the horses quickly learn to ignore. The horses and riders also move through yellow caution tape, walk up and down ramps, and feel how a ramp moves under their hooves. Most importantly, the horses get used to people walking and running up to them, charging at them, and even grabbing them.

For their protection, police horses may wear special equipment. Horses who work in cities may wear special horseshoes that won't slip on concrete. Their saddles are usually lighter in weight than regular saddles, and the pads under the saddles are often thicker so the horse's back is more comfortable. If the horse may be facing an angry crowd, she may even wear armor to protect her face and body.

Pulling Heavy Loads

Horses are very strong, especially the types of horses bred to pull heavy loads. These horses, called *draft horses,* are bigger and heavier than horses used for riding. Their necks are thick, and their shoulders are strong. Their bodies have room for a large heart and lungs so they can work hard. And their legs and hooves are heavy.

Horses have pulled wagons, carts, carriages, plows, and other loads for many years. However, humans have not always been kind to the horses who worked so hard. Henry Bergh was born in 1813 and was the son of a rich ship builder. He served as a diplomat in Russia, and was horrified at the way working horses were beaten by their drivers. When he came home to New York City, he saw the same thing. Often the horses were overworked and underfed, and they were forced to pull loads that were much too heavy for them.

So Henry dedicated his life to making the world a better place, first for horses, and then for dogs, cats, and all other animals. He founded the ASPCA in 1866. The next year, the ASPCA had an ambulance for horses working in New York. A few years later, a sling had been invented that could support weak or injured horses until they recovered. (This is important because a horse must be on her feet most of the time; if a horse lies down for too long, she will die.) When Henry passed away in 1888, the idea that people needed to protect animals rather than be cruel to them was gaining popularity. Henry had made a huge difference in the lives of animals.

Although the first American car was manufactured in the late 1880s, horses were still the primary means of transportation until the 1920s and '30s. Over many years, steam locomotives, cars, trucks, motorcycles, and other vehicles gradually replaced the horse.

Today, many horses still work at jobs where they are required to pull wagons or carriages. However, people today are more aware of how much weight a horse should be asked to pull. The horses are also fed a good diet and see a veterinarian regularly, and a farrier checks their hooves regularly. Even so, laws are needed to protect horses from poor conditions, such as in big cities where cars and buses pollute the air horses must breathe.

Training has changed over the years, too. Instead of being made to work by being hit with a stick or a whip, horses are trained with treats, petting, and soft words. They are asked to work for us, not forced to. This makes a big difference.

Budweiser Clydesdales

The most famous draft horses in the world are the Budweiser company Clydesdales. These horses are seen in parades, at special events, in holiday television commercials, and, most famously, in Super Bowl advertisements. Eight huge draft horses pulling a beautiful wagon, their coats gleaming with good health and their harnesses shining, catch everyone's attention.

Clydesdale horses were developed in Scotland, where they worked on farms. In the 1800s, Scottish immigrants brought the first Clydesdales to America. August Busch Jr. bought a team of these beautiful horses in 1933 as a gift for his father, August Busch Sr. His dad saw the horses pulling a red, white, and gold wagon loaded with cases of beer from their Budweiser brewery, and his dad was thrilled. The horses became both useful employees and wildly popular ambassadors for their company.

Today there are five eight-horse hitches (teams) of Budweiser Clydesdales in the United States. The teams travel to special events, walk in parades, and perform in commercials. More than a thousand requests are made for the horses to perform each year. The horses also make special appearances at hospitals and senior citizens' facilities. The teams are based in St. Louis, Missouri; Menifee, California; San Diego, California; Merrimack, New Hampshire; and San Antonio, Texas.

Budweiser Clydesdales must be at least 4 years old, be six feet tall at the top of the shoulders, and weigh between 1,800 and 2,300 pounds. All the horses are bay (red-gold in color) and have four white stockings (white hair on their feet and legs), a blaze of white on the face, and a black mane and tail.

Although each team consists of eight horses pulling a wagon, there are actually twelve horses assigned to each team. This allows time for each horse to relax and have a break from work.

Matt, Marty, and Chris are the three horses used most often as actors in Budweiser commercials. Because these commercials are shown during the Super Bowl, the horses are recognized wherever they go. Depending on what they have to do in the commercial, it usually takes three to four weeks to train the horses to perform their tasks.

Misty Pulls a Cart

Misty is a brown and white mixed-breed pony. She's about 10 years old, and she enjoys pulling her little two-wheeled cart. Her person, Sylvia, says, "Misty is too small for anyone except a small child to ride, and she was getting bored just hanging out in the pasture, so we taught her to pull a small cart. The cart is lightweight, even when I ride in it, and she pulls it easily."

To introduce Misty to the cart, Sylvia walked Misty around the cart, letting her sniff it, see it from all sides, and satisfy her curiosity about it. Then, while Sylvia walked Misty on a lead rope, she asked a couple of friends to pull the cart themselves, each of them lifting one of the shafts (the side poles that help the horse stop and steer the cart). Sylvia walked Misty behind the cart, to the side of it, and in front of it, letting her get used to the moving cart, the noises it makes, and the sight of it. During all of this training, Sylvia talked to Misty, calming her when she was nervous and offering her treats for good behavior.

At different training sessions, Sylvia introduced Misty to the harness that she would wear to pull the cart. Sylvia put one piece on Misty at a time, letting the pony get used to the feel of it. Then she added another piece. When Misty was comfortable with the harness, Sylvia then walked her while she was wearing it so the pony could get used to the feel of the harness on her body.

Step by step, the training continued over several weeks. If at any time Misty seemed worried, Sylvia wouldn't push her or get angry. She would simply slow the training down, try to discover what was bothering the pony, and then help Misty work through it.

About three months after her training began, Misty took Sylvia for a ride around town in her cart. While Sylvia rode in the cart and guided Misty using the reins, Misty pranced in front of her cart. Sylvia says, "She was so proud of herself! She pranced and high stepped, and she neighed and nickered, telling the whole world how special she was. It was a lot of fun."

We Love to Watch Horses

e love to watch horses. Perhaps it's their grace, their strength, or their beauty. It doesn't seem to matter whether horses are working, performing, or running free. This has made them very popular in the entertainment business. Horses can be seen in movies, on television, and in commercials.

Cavalia

One show that features horses is called Cavalia. This show was started by a Canadian producer and a French horse trainer. It uses sixty-four horses, plus a crew of performers and support people who care for the horses. They travel around the world giving multimedia shows.

The breeds of horses in the show include Lusitanos (a Spanish breed), Quarter Horses (American horses used by cowboys), Belgian draft horses (from Europe), and Appaloosas (a

Native American breed). Throughout the show, the horses show off their training. It also has segments where the horses perform natural actions. They can run, play, and even come to their trainers for stroking and petting.

The star of the show, Templado, is a white Lusitano stallion. He is elegant, graceful, and incredibly well trained. His mane is long, reaching to his knees.

The horses of Cavalia practice their training for one hour each day and get two hours every day to go outside and play. They perform for only ten minutes each per show. More than one horse is taught each part in the show so that each horse can take a day off.

The show is wonderful and demonstrates the powerful relationship that can develop between a horse and her trainer.

Horses Who Dance

Some of the most famous horses used for entertainment didn't actually begin as performers. The Lipizzaner horses who perform in shows all over the world today are descended from special horses bred for military use in the Austrian Empire in the 1500s. During battles, the Lipizzaner horses were taught to perform moves such as rearing (lifting their front legs off the ground) to scare the enemy. The horses were also taught to be calm when facing danger.

In 1735, the Spanish Riding School was begun in Vienna, Austria, so that both the Lipizzaner horses and their riders could learn the right way to perform the special skills that were needed for the military. It is called *Spanish* because the horses are descended from Spanish horses and because they ride in a classical style that was developed in Spain. Only Lipizzaner horses are allowed in the Spanish Riding School, because they were the only horses who showed the style, strength, and bravery that was needed.

In the Spanish Riding School today, the horses are taught how to perform dance moves that are similar to what the horses were taught hundreds of years ago when the school first began. All these moves are related to those used by the military in battle, although the horses do not work in the military anymore.

The moves are also much like those the horses would use when playing with other horses. One move is to lift the front legs high and balance on the hind legs. Horses will do this when playing out in a field. But to do it with a rider and when asked takes a lot of training and practice. Another move asks the horse to jump completely off the ground and then kick out with the back legs before landing. The dance moves the horses perform while jumping in the air are called *airs above the ground*.

To do these dances, the Lipizzaner horses must be very strong. And they are. They are compact, powerful horses with strong hips that help them perform the movements in their dances. Their necks are arched and their faces are friendly. These horses are naturally graceful. Almost all Lipizzaners are gray horses. Gray horses are born dark, and as they grow older they get lighter in color. Older horses are often all white. Once in awhile, a Lipizzaner of another color is born, but this is unusual.

Today, Lipizzaner horses are rare. There are only 3,000 known in the world. They are still trained at the Spanish Riding School in Vienna, and those horses perform shows to support the riding school. Books have been written about them, and they have starred in a few movies. People from all over the world know who the dancing white horses are. Some other Lipizzaner horses who are also trained in the classical style perform regularly in Europe and in America in groups such as the Royal Lipizzans.

There's More That Horses Do

Horses have been companions and working animals for thousands of years. People have used them to travel long distances, carry loads, and pull things. There have been all kinds of variations of these three basic jobs. Today, the work that horses do is still based on these tasks.

Cowboys!

What would a cowboy be without his horse? Unfortunately for the local environment, many cowboys in the American West now use all-terrain vehicles and off-road motorcycles. But some still prefer a horse. Motorcycles might be fun,

but they aren't good company! They can also damage the land they ride over. The horse's senses can alert the cowboy to the presence of a stranded calf, a predator, or dangers such as a rattlesnake.

The word *cowboy* refers to the people—men and women—who work with livestock, primarily in the American West. Cowboys make sure their livestock, which may include horses, sheep, and goats, but is primarily cattle, are well cared for, safe, and healthy. During the course of his day, a cowboy may need to move his animals from one pasture to another, bring in a group of animals to check their health, or vaccinate them to prevent disease. The cowboy's horse may be his primary means of transportation, as well as his best friend.

Search and Rescue

Search-and-rescue volunteers have many vehicles to choose from to conduct searches, from their feet to helicopters to boats and snowmobiles, depending on the search and the terrain. But many search-and-rescue experts like to use their own horses. Not only can they cover more ground quickly on horseback, but also the horses seem to know what the job is and will alert (by looking or flicking their ears) to a person who seems out of place.

Volunteer search-and-rescue people and their horses (as well as dogs) are very important. Although many police officers are trained in search-and-rescue work, there are never enough officers to do all that is needed. So a search might be organized and run by a police officer, but volunteers often do much of the actual searching. With many volunteer searchers out looking for the person or people who are missing, there are many more chances for the people to be found.

Very Special Horses

Some very special Miniature Horses have a different kind of special job. They serve as guide horses for people who cannot see. The Guide Horse Foundation oversees the selection and training of these tiny horses. All guide horses must be less than twenty-six inches tall at the shoulders; any larger and the person would have difficulty incorporating the horse into his or her lifestyle. A larger horse might work well but couldn't take an elevator! The horse must also be healthy, strong, and able to physically do the work that will be asked of her. Once the horse completes her training, she will work with her person in all the situations a guide dog might, including guiding her human partner down a busy street or riding the escalator at the shopping mall.

Donkeys Work, Too

Donkeys are a cousin of horses, and they work hard for people, too. Some donkeys are almost as big as horses, but most are closer in size to ponies. In America, donkeys are also called *burros* (*burro* is Spanish for "donkey").

Donkeys are very strong for their size and were often used to carry loads on their backs. During the California Gold Rush in the 1800s, many of the gold miners used donkeys to carry all their supplies.

Donkeys are also known for being sure-footed, which means they don't stumble. They can walk over uneven ground and climb rocky hills, and because they are careful where they step, they don't fall or hurt themselves.

Many people think donkeys are stubborn because it's hard to force a donkey to do something she doesn't want to do. Training a donkey needs to be done with kindness, sweet words, and a treat or two. Once a donkey is your friend, though, she will do anything for you.

Fruitcake is a donkey who works on a cattle ranch in Southern California. He is gray with black on his ears and a white nose. Along with several other donkeys, Fruitcake carries supplies for the cowboys while they take care of the cattle.

Although many cowboys now use trucks, the cowboys on this ranch like to ride horses and use donkeys to carry supplies. John, one of the cowboys, says, "Trucks are okay, but it's hard to talk to one. My horse, Sandy, listens when I talk, and so does Fruitcake. Fruitcake even talks back!" Donkeys don't whinny and neigh as horses do. They bray with a loud "heehaw!"

Each summer, when the weather begins to warm up, the donkeys and the cowboys' horses take a vacation. They travel by truck to a small ranch in the California mountains. It's cooler there, and the horses and donkeys can relax, graze in the pastures, and enjoy themselves. After two months, they go back to work.

Mighty Mules

A mule has a horse for a mother and a donkey for a father. Mules can be smaller or larger than horses, depending on what breed the mother horse was. Mules look like donkeys because they have long ears and small hooves. But they also look like horses, with a body shape and hair like a horse. Also like horses, mules can be colors other than gray. Mules have the patience and sure-footedness of donkeys and the energy and courage of horses.

A mule can work hard, pull heavy loads, and carry a rider for long distances. But like a donkey, a mule won't work so hard that she hurts herself, as horses sometimes do. A mule will stop before that happens.

Sierra is a mule whose mother was an Appaloosa horse. Like an Appaloosa, Sierra's skin is brown, but her hair is mostly white with brown spots. Her long ears are brown, her hips are brown, and the bottom of her legs just above her hooves is brown. Sierra's pet parent, Jeff, leads horseback riding tours. People who live in cities can visit his ranch to ride horses.

He says he likes to ride Sierra on these horseback riding trips because she keeps them both safe. She watches where she steps, stops before she gets too tired, and won't let him load her with more than she can carry.

Mules played an important part in America's growth. Many mules were used on farms and to pull wagons across the plains. Today, mules still work hard, but most are used for riding. People who like mules have formed clubs so they can do fun things together. For example, the Alberta Donkey and Mule Club, in Alberta, Canada, hosts a variety of events, including trail rides, training clinics, shows, and participation in local parades.

5 Respecting and Caring for Our Caring for Our Working Partners

No matter whether our working partner is a dog, a cat, a horse, or a donkey, he deserves to be treated well, be fed the best foods, and receive the best veterinary care. When he's working, he should be asked to do a job that he's able to do and never asked to do more than he's capable of. When he's tired, he needs to rest. And when he can no longer work, he deserves a chance to retire with love and care for the rest of his life.

Our working animal friends depend on us to keep them safe, to care for them, and to protect them throughout their lives, from birth through old age. When they spend their lives with us, working for us, we must do our best for them.

Where Do Working Animals Come From?

Working animals can come from many different places. Today, there is a huge demand for animals who can work with people and perform their jobs well. To meet this need, many groups that train working animals, such as service dog organizations, also breed them. Some other examples of working animals who are specially bred for the work they do include the Lipizzaner horses and the Budweiser Clydesdales.

Not all working animals are bred specifically for their jobs. Someone might donate a well-loved family pet to a working dog group. A dog breeder may offer puppies with working potential to a service dog school or a search-and-rescue team. A horse breeder might offer a young horse to police department trainers because the horse has the qualities the police department is looking for. People who train and work with animals also buy them from responsible breeders who have a reputation for producing healthy, well-behaved animals.

Some animals who now work hard at their jobs were found in local shelters. They may never have had a loving home, or they may have lost their home. Many people who train working animals look for homeless animals to train. They like the idea of saving an animal's life, and they have found that there are many very nice animals at shelters—animals who need homes and jobs to do. Many dogs and cats in show business, for example, come from shelters.

Guide Dogs for the Blind

Guide Dogs for the Blind in San Rafael, California, trains dogs to assist people who can't see. Because the trainers look for very special dogs—dogs who are healthy, intelligent, kind, and social, and love to work for praise—they began their own breeding program.

Labrador Retrievers are the most common breed the group uses, although they also train some Golden Retrievers. They also breed Labrador Retriever–Golden Retriever crosses (one parent is a Lab and the other is a Golden).

In the breeding program, they try to produce dogs who have the traits they need, as well as dogs who are large enough to assist an adult. At the same time, the dog can't be too big, because the person who can't see may need to ride the bus or train to work, and the dog needs to be able to fit in easily.

The dog also needs to be able to work in different climates. The person needing assistance may live in North Dakota, where winters are very cold, or in Texas, where summers are hot. A dog with a medium-length coat can handle different climates more easily.

All the puppies (and of course their mothers) are cared for by a team of experts, including veterinarians and volunteers who enjoy working with puppies.

Budweiser Clydesdales

The huge horses who pull the beautiful wagons in parades and commercials are specially bred for the job. Clydesdales are big draft horses who weigh between 1,800 and 2,300 pounds when fully grown. Smaller horses couldn't do the job that these big horses do.

Several farms raise horses as a part of the Budweiser Clydesdale breeding program. Grant's Farm in St. Louis, Missouri, is one of those farms. The farm has several pastures surrounded by white fences where horses can run, play, or graze on the green grass. Automatic waterers ensure that clean water is always available. There are three barns for shelter, and each year fifteen foals are born on Grant's Farm.

The babies remain at the farm until they are 2 to 3 years old. At that age, they begin their training. The training progresses slowly so the young horses don't feel as if they're being rushed. Horses are never assigned to a working hitch until they are at least 4 years old.

Royal Canadian Mounted Police Horses

The Royal Canadian Mounted Police has its own breeding program, too, located in Ontario, Canada. It breeds horses who are very athletic, comfortable to ride, and easily trained.

The horses of the Royal Canadian Mounted Police no longer work as police horses. Instead, they walk in parades and appear in other ceremonies. In addition, the officers and horses perform in a famous show called the Musical Ride. In the Musical Ride, thirty-two horses and riders perform intricate drill team steps and movements to music. People come from all over the world to see this show.

The Horses at Arlington National Cemetery

The horses who pull the wagons for the funerals at Arlington National Cemetery are not as big as the Budweiser Clydesdales, but they are still big horses. They weigh from 1,250 to 1,400 pounds, and they must be strong to do their work.

The horses at Arlington, who work with the U.S. Army's Caisson Platoon, are not bred by the Army, but instead come from three farms. One of the farms is in Iowa and is owned by Robert. He says, "Two of the horses I have trained for the Army to work at Arlington are Major and Ted. When they finish their training, Major and Ted will join eighteen other horses from my farm."

Shelter Dogs

Texas Hearing and Service Dogs in Dripping Springs, Texas, adopts dogs from shelters and rescue groups. The dogs are trained to be assistance dogs for people who need help. Once the dogs are adopted, they are taught basic obedience skills such as sit, lie down, stay, come, and heel. Then they are taught the specific skills they might need in their future job. Some dogs learn to pick up items from the floor, while others learn to alert a person who cannot hear to a siren or a doorbell.

Abandoned Horses

Prince Charming is a reddish-gold mixed-breed horse. Today he works as a riding horse for children with disabilities, but three years ago he was abandoned. Luckily, someone who was familiar with scared horses saw him and was able to catch him, calm the frightened horse, and get him some food and water.

A local rescue group took him in and named him Prince Charming because even though he was frightened, he still had good manners and never tried to hurt anyone. His good manners also made him an excellent horse for the children's riding program, where he has found a home.

Working Animals Deserve the Best Care

Animals who work for people deserve the best care we can give them. They can't care for themselves, so they rely on us. When cared for well, our working friends can live long, happy lives with us.

Water

We all need water to stay alive. Without enough water, we would soon get sick and die. This is true of both people and animals.

Water should be offered to working animals several times each day, including before work, during breaks from work, and during meals. When work is done for the day, the animal should be allowed to have free access to water for the rest of the day.

Water needs can change, too. If an animal is working very hard, he may need more water than normal. He will also need more water when the weather is hot. The people who work and care for working animals learn to watch their partners and know when to offer more water.

Police officers usually carry water in the patrol car for their patrol dog partners. Search-and-rescue dog handlers carry water with them on searches and during training, and water is always available back at the search headquarters.

Kate's talented mixed-breed dog, Walter, does lots of tricks during his therapy dog visits. Kate carries a foldable plastic bowl and a bottle of water so she can offer him a drink often.

It's harder to carry enough water for horses, donkeys, and mules to drink, because they can drink gallons of water every day. But the people who work with these large animals know where water is available and how often their animal partner needs to stop and take a drink.

Food

We are healthier, get sick less often, and have more energy for work and play when we eat good foods. Animals, including working animals, are the same way.

Every animal has different needs when it comes to food. For example, some horses are able to work and play while eating grass in a pasture with just a little added grain (oats, barley, or flaxseed, for example). Other horses need different foods.

Scooter, the Miniature Horse you met in chapter 4, can't graze on grass too much. His human mom, Nicole, says, "Scooter can have problems with his feet, so I have to watch his diet carefully. He eats good-quality hay (which is dried grass and contains less fat than growing grass), just a little bit of grain with some vitamins and minerals, and then he can graze for an hour or so each day." If Scooter grazes too much, he tends to gain too much weight, which is not good for his health and is even worse for his feet.

Terry's Icelandic Horse, Ari, can graze as much as he wants. He doesn't tend to gain weight when grazing. He also gets good-quality hay every morning and evening and some grain each morning.

The Budweiser Clydesdales are huge horses who work very hard. The people who care for them say, "When working, each horse will drink thirty gallons of water each day and eat twenty-five quarts of whole grains and vitamins, as well as sixty pounds of hay." That's a lot of food and water!

Dogs and cats also need good-quality foods. Both dogs and cats are meat eaters—unlike horses, who eat only plants. That means dogs and cats need good foods made from meats. Bubba, the therapy cat you met in chapter 3, eats good-quality canned and dry cat foods. Although his favorite foods are made from fish, he is fed a variety of foods—chicken, beef, and different kinds of fish—so that he gets everything he needs from his food.

Walter, the trick dog, eats a good dry food every day, morning and evening. Kate says, "Because I use treats while training Walter to do his tricks, I make sure I use good foods as his training treats. I will use bits of cooked chicken or beef or tiny pieces of cheese. I avoid any treats with sugar in them, because sugar is not good for Walter."

Sled dogs, who work very hard in cold conditions, need lots of high-calorie foods (meats and fats) to be able to work as hard as they do. The people who work with them feed them special diets to make sure they get all the energy they need from their food.

Rest

Even the strongest working animals need time to relax, rest, and sleep. That's another way in which animals are just like us. If we don't have enough time away from work, we may hurt ourselves because we aren't being careful. When we're tired, we can also get angry or grouchy. We don't work as well as we normally do. If we don't get the rest or sleep we need for a long time, we may even get sick. Our animal partners are the same way.

Police dogs usually work with their human partners on the same schedule. That means the dog will work an eight-hour shift four or five days a week. Although the dog may work hard when searching for someone or sniffing for drugs, he isn't working hard all the time. The dog may spend time sleeping while his human partner writes reports or interviews people. The dog also has time to relax in the police car while his human partner drives.

Therapy dogs and cats usually visit schools, day-care centers, nursing homes, or hospitals for an hour at a time, once or twice a week. Although this seems like a short period of time, the animals are usually more than ready for a nap afterward. Visiting people can be hard work!

Friendship

Although Flea is a visiting therapy cat and enjoys seeing people, his favorite person is the person he lives with, Paul. Every evening when Paul gets home from work, Flea follows him from room to room, talking to him with tiny meows. Paul says, "I think Flea is telling me about his day—the birds he watched at the bird feeder outside his window, the good breakfast he had, and the wonderful nap he took while lying in the sun." As soon as Paul sits down in his recliner in the living room, Flea is up on his lap, purring loudly.

Often, animals work hard because they like the work they do. Search-and-rescue dogs, for example, love to use their ability to follow a scent and often do this even while playing. But our working animal friends also work hard because they want to please us and because they enjoy our company. In return, it's important that we give them our time and attention.

When we spend time with them, we can groom them, check their bodies for any problems, and care for them. We can also relax with them, letting the cat purr on our lap, the dog sleep at our feet, or the horse graze nearby as we take a nap in a lawn chair.

Play is also relaxing and is great fun for us and our animal friends. Most dogs love to bring back a ball we have thrown. Most dogs also enjoy having their tummies rubbed. Cats like to play with a toy on the end of a pole, and some cats will even bring back toys that are thrown.

83

Many horses like to play by running around and kicking up their heels, but some like to play with toys. You met Raz, Petra's Morgan Horse, in chapter 4. He likes to pick up an orange traffic cone and toss it around. Once he throws it, he'll chase after it, grab it in his teeth, shake his head, and throw it again. Petra leans on the bars of his corral and cheers him on as he plays.

Companionship

Although not all cats like the company of other cats (some like to be the only cat in the house), most dogs and horses enjoy the companionship of other dogs and horses. When possible, it's relaxing for a working animal to spend time with others of his kind. He can then relax, play if he wants, or just enjoy their company. Just as we like spending time with friends, so do our working animal friends.

It's important for us to understand the habits of our animal partners' wild ancestors, because that helps us understand what our partners need. In the wild, dogs live in groups called packs and horses live in groups called herds. So when we look at horses and dogs, we know that they need the companionship of other animals.

Terry, who does park patrols with her Icelandic Horse, Ari, has another horse at home, too, so Ari has company when Terry can't be with him. Petra keeps a friend's pony at her house so that her horse, Raz, and the pony can keep each other company.

Charlie, a Labrador Retriever search-and-rescue dog, has a Lab mix best friend at home. Ranger, a German Shepherd police dog, goes home each night with his police officer partner, who has another dog at home. Ranger and Jessie, a Beagle mix, enjoy each other's company and play in the backyard every evening.

Health and Veterinary Care

Our animal partners can't care for themselves, so they need us to care for them. Caring for them means doing all that is needed to make sure they remain healthy. If they are injured or sick, we must do what is needed to help them get well.

Grooming

Cats are very good about keeping themselves clean and neat, but they need some help. Paul says, "Flea has a short coat that always looks very nice. But I brush it weekly to keep him looking and feeling his best. Brushing also pulls out the dead hairs so that Flea doesn't swallow them when he grooms himself. That helps prevent him from later coughing up hairballs (wads of swallowed hair)." The grooming needs of most cats include:

- Regular brushing and combing
- Preventing fleas and ticks, and removing any found on the cat
- Trimming the nails
- Checking to make sure the ears are clean, and gently cleaning them if they're dirty
- Brushing the cat's teeth or taking him to a veterinarian for regular cleanings
- Bathing the cat if he gets into something really dirty or dangerous (many cats go their whole lives without ever needing a bath)

Caleb, the therapy dog you met in chapter 2, gets a bath before each visit, so he's clean and neat. He's also brushed well, his nails are trimmed short, and his ears are cleaned. The people he visits don't want to pet a dirty dog! In addition, a dog who is not well groomed may scratch someone with tender skin. If the dog has fleas, he could bring those fleas into the hospital or nursing home, and that could cause many problems when the fleas start biting people. The grooming needs of most dogs include:

- Regular brushing and combing
- Preventing fleas and ticks, and removing any found on the dog
- Trimming the nails
- Checking to make sure the ears are clean, and gently cleaning them if they're dirty
- Bathing the dog if he's dirty or if it's needed for work
- Giving the dog a haircut if it's needed for work or if the breed of dog is normally given a haircut
- Brushing the dog's teeth or taking him to a veterinarian for regular cleanings

Scooter, the therapy horse, gets bathed and brushed before each visit to the nursing home. His mane and tail, which are both very long, are also combed out so there are no tangles, and his hooves are cleaned and polished so they are shiny. When he visits, his brown and white coat is shiny and bright. The grooming needs of most horses include:

- Regular bathing and brushing
- Combing the tail and mane
- Clipping the coat for comfort if it's needed for work or due to the weather
- Checking the hooves and cleaning them
- Making sure flies and mosquitoes are not bothering the horse and taking care to prevent them if they are

Horses also need a farrier to come care for their hooves. Horses' hooves grow all the time, just as our fingernails do. And, just like our fingernails, hooves need to be trimmed. So a farrier visits a horse every six weeks and trims the hooves so the horse can walk comfortably.

Some horses wear shoes on their hooves. The shoes are nailed through the hard part of the hooves. It sounds like this would hurt, but it doesn't. That's because the hard part of the hoof is just like the part of your nail that extends past your fingers—it doesn't have any feeling. The shoes help protect the horse's feet from being damaged by hard or rough ground. Horses who walk on streets, sidewalks, or gravel wear softer shoes—like hard rubber—that help keep them from slipping. Horses who walk on dirt or grass may wear steel shoes that help them grip the softer ground.

Veterinary Care

Working animals need routine veterinary care to help keep them healthy. A veterinarian is a doctor who cares for animals, just as your doctor cares for you. When you go in for a checkup, your doctor looks at you, takes your temperature, and asks questions about your health. If there's a problem, he or she helps solve it. A veterinarian does the same thing for our animal friends.

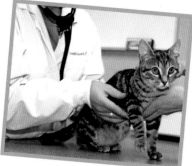

During a checkup, the veterinarian can look the animal over, listen to his heart and lung sounds, check and possibly even clean the teeth, and give any needed vaccinations (shots) to prevent diseases. Most veterinarians recommend that all companion and working animals get a checkup each year. However, if the animal regularly works very hard as do police horses, police dogs, sled dogs, and horses pulling heavy loads, then veterinary checkups should be done more often.

Veterinarians also suggest that working animals go to the vet's office any time the animal hurts himself or appears sick or acts different than usual. That way, any necessary treatment can begin right away.

Keeping Them Safe

Those people who work with animals must also keep their working partners safe. That can be hard sometimes because danger is often a part of the job. Police officers and their dog partners face danger daily. So to protect their dogs, most police officers have bulletproof vests that the dogs can wear while on duty. There are even pieces of armor that police horses can wear for protection—especially to protect their faces.

Search-and-rescue dog handlers make safety a part of their training. The dogs are taught how to walk slowly and carefully through broken pieces of concrete, on broken boards, and around pieces of coiled wire. The dogs are also taught to avoid snakes so they won't be bitten by poisonous ones. Many search-and-rescue dogs wear dog boots to protect their feet.

Safety is a part of horse training, too. Horses who work in crowds are taught to be calm and to stand still when people crowd around them. Park patrol horses and search-and-rescue horses learn to avoid snakes. They also learn to walk around or step over obstacles safely so they don't hurt themselves or drop their riders.

Therapy animals—dogs, cats, horses, and any other animal who may participate in this activity—must also be kept safe. Their human partners are taught to watch their pets all the time during visits and not to look away. That way if someone hugs a cat or a tiny dog too hard, his handler can quickly get the animal out of that situation. If someone tries to poke a dog's eye, kick a horse, or pull a cat's tail, the handler must step in immediately. The human partner will remove the animal from danger. If possible, this can become a good time to teach people how to treat animals kindly.

When safety is a part of a working animal's training and when the human partner keeps his animal partner's safety in mind all the time, there is less chance of the animal (or human!) getting hurt.

Ongoing Training

Working animals, just like people who work, must constantly practice their skills. It's important, then, that training be an ongoing process for all working animals. Working animals are more motivated to work and happiest to do well at their jobs when they earn a paycheck, just like we do. For animals, that is usually food treats, their favorite toy, or playtime with their human partner. When working animals are trained this way, they see their job as fun and not boring.

Dogs who are a part of the Beagle Brigade for the Department of Agriculture often participate in training sessions. The dog and handler train using various foods, such as fruits, plants, or meats. The dog is taught to sit when he finds these foods in boxes, packages, or luggage, and the dog is always rewarded with a special treat when he finds the foods. This training keeps his skills sharp for when he's working.

Police officers and their dogs train regularly, as well. The officer may set up a training search for the dog to find someone or may hide an object for the dog to find. They also practice obedience skills such as sit, down, stay, and come.

Training also helps keep a working animal safe. A well-trained animal will do what his human partner asks of him—which can be important both to his job and to his safety. Also, when animal and person are used to working with each other, the handler knows how the animal will react and can take steps to protect him.

When It's Time for a Change

Cats who live in the house and are well cared for often live to be 17 to 20 years old. Some live even longer. Well-loved and cared for dogs can live 13 to 15 years. Many horses live to be 25 or even 30 years old. The working careers of our friends are definitely not that long, though. Just as people deserve to retire and relax when they get older or when they don't enjoy working anymore, so do our animal friends.

Most working cats remain right where they are, where they live, and just bask in the sun a little more. Flea continued doing therapy visits until he was 16 years old. Paul stopped taking him on visits when he noticed that Flea was sleeping more and was less excited about his work.

Dogs are usually ready for retirement when their bodies begin showing their age. Maybe the dog is stiff and sore in the morning or can't jump into the car anymore. An older search-and-rescue dog may no longer be able to search all day, and a therapy dog might just get tired of being petted all the time. Many dogs try to keep doing their jobs long after they should have quit, so it's the human's responsibility to pay attention to his working animal partner and do what's best.

When a guide dog trained through Guide Dogs of America is ready to retire, he can remain with his blind person as a pet, or he can go back to the Guide Dogs group. Sometimes these dogs are taken back in by the people who raised them as puppies. Guide Dogs of America also has a waiting list of people who would like to adopt these older, very well trained dogs. No matter who takes them in, the dogs are treasured members of a family for as long as they live.

Canine Companions for Independence, which trains dogs to help people who need physical assistance, has a similar program. Retired dogs or dogs who don't pass the training program or health screening are all called *career change dogs.* They can go back to the people who raised them or are offered for adoption.

When the dogs who are a part of the Beagle Brigade for the U.S. Department of Agriculture show a lack of interest in working or seem more tired than normal, they may be offered a vacation from work. But after working for six to ten years, a dog may be ready to retire. The working Beagle's handler may choose to adopt him. If the handler does not or cannot adopt him, there is a waiting list of people ready to adopt these dogs.

In 2000, President Bill Clinton signed legislation allowing military dog handlers to adopt the retired dogs they had worked with. The law was known as Robby's Law, after an 11-year-old Belgian Malinois who had worked in the army. When Robby retired, the soldier who had handled him wanted to take Robby home to live with him. But the law said military dogs were "equipment" and could not be given away. Many groups worked to change the law, and Robby and other dogs like him can now enjoy their well-earned retirement in the company of their longtime companions.

Retirement programs are available for working horses, too. Mill Creek Farm in Gainesville, Florida, takes in many retired horses, including police horses, park patrol horses, and horses who have worked in therapy riding programs. Some of their recent arrivals include Dewey and Cody, who were both police horses; Collier, a park patrol horse; and Charlie, who was a therapy riding horse.

The San Francisco Society for the Prevention of Cruelty to Animals supports all the horses who retire from the San Francisco Police Department. They are given free stabling, food, farrier visits, grooming, and veterinary care for as long as they live. The horses live on a ranch in Sonoma County where they can graze on green grass, run and play, or just sleep in the sun.

Resources

Here are some organizations related to the working animals mentioned in this book. You can visit their Web sites to learn more about them.

Arlington National Cemetery
www.arlingtoncemetery.net
Ceremonies at Arlington National Cemetery are somber events but are a comfort to the families. Here is more information about the cemetery and the horses who participate in the funerals there.

ASPCA
www.aspca.org
This site has information about the ASPCA's programs. Also included is historical information about how the organization was founded by Henry Bergh in 1866.

The Beagle Brigade
www.aphis.usda.gov/lpa/pubs/detdog3.html
The United States Department of Agriculture's Beagle Brigade makes a vital contribution to our national security.

The Budweiser Clydesdales
www.grantsfarm.com/ClydesdaleStables.htm
www.thehorse.com/ViewArticle.aspx?ID=8516
These huge horses and their sparkling wagon are famous around the world.

Canine Companions for Independence
www.caninecompanions.org
CCI trains, evaluates, and certifies service dogs to help people in a variety of ways.

Cavalia
www.cavalia.net
Learn all about the show, the horses who perform in it, and the trainer who supervises the horses.

The Delta Society
www.deltasociety.org
This group evaluates and certifies animals to do therapy work.

Foundation for Pet-Provided Therapy
www.loveonaleash.org
This group also evaluates and certifies therapy pets.

Guide Dogs of America
www.guidedogsofamerica.org
This group provides guide dogs for the visually impaired.

Guide Dogs for the Blind
www.guidedogs.com
Read all about these wonderfully talented and dedicated dogs who help the blind.

Guide Horse Foundation
www.guidehorse.org
This organization trains and tests Miniature Horses for use as guide horses.

Intermountain Therapy Animals
www.therapyanimals.org
This group provides animal-assisted therapy in a wide variety of areas. They started the READ program, which is the first program in which children read to dogs.

The Lipizzaner Stallions
www.lipizzaner.com
This site tells you all about these wonderful horses from the Spanish Riding School.

Mill Creek Farm in Florida
www.millcreekfarm.org
The Retirement Home for Horses gives lifetime care to rescued horses, horses retired from government service, horses used by handicapped riding programs, and others.

North American Riding for the Handicapped Association
www.narha.org
NARHA provides guidelines for riding instructors and also certifies riding programs.

Royal Canadian Mounted Police
www.rcmp-grc.gc.ca/index_e.htm
As this Canadian police force's name suggests, they originated on horseback. Learn more about the famous Mounties and the Musical Ride, their drill team performance.

San Francisco SPCA
www.sfspca.org
Read all about the organization, including its special program for retired police horses.

Texas Hearing and Service Dogs
www.servicedogs.org
This organization trains and certifies dogs to assist people in a variety of ways.

Therapy Dogs Inc.
www.therapydogs.com
This group provides registration, support, and insurance for members who are involved in volunteer animal-assisted activities.

Vest-A-Dog
www.vestadog.com
This is a nationwide foundation committed to providing bulletproof vests to law enforcement dogs throughout the country.

About the Authors

Liz Palika

Liz Palika, CPDT, CABC, has been working with animals her whole life. She writes books and magazine articles about dogs, cats, and reptiles. She trains dogs in obedience, agility, herding, and other dog sports. And she works with dogs, cats, and horses in volunteer therapy work. Liz and her husband, Paul, share their home with three Australian Shepherds—Riker, Bashir, and Archer—and three cats—Xena, Pumpkin, and Squash. They also participated in reptile rescue for many years, and have a 25-year-old leopard tortoise named Pearl and several other reptiles.

Dr. Katherine A. Miller

Katherine Miller, PhD, CAAB, CPDT, is the assistant science advisor at the ASPCA and is a certified applied animal behaviorist and a certified pet dog trainer. Her love of animals began at around 6 years of age. Since then she has lived happily together with a variety of animal companions, including dogs, cats, hamsters, birds, mice, a rat, a rabbit, a hermit crab, and fish. Kat also has a strong interest in poultry. She currently lives in New Jersey with her husband, Josh, cats named Grover and Ivy, and a newly adopted dog named Stella.

About the ASPCA

The American Society for the Prevention of Cruelty to Animals (ASPCA) was founded in 1866 by a wealthy man from New York City named Henry Bergh. Henry first got the idea of devoting his life to protecting animals when he was serving as a diplomat in Russia. While riding in a fancy horse-drawn coach, Henry saw a peasant beating a lame cart horse on the side of the road. The horse was injured and couldn't put weight on one of his legs, but the peasant was beating him to force him to continue pulling the cart. Henry ordered the man to stop. Russian peasants did not dare argue with noblemen, so the man did as he was told. In that moment Henry Bergh felt great joy at being able to help a suffering animal.

Henry resigned his diplomatic post and returned to the United States where he worked tirelessly to set up a society to protect animals and to convince the New York State Legislature to pass a law making it a crime to beat and overwork animals. The legislature not only passed a law but gave the ASPCA the police power to enforce the new law throughout the state. The ASPCA was the first animal protection organization in the Western Hemisphere, and Henry Bergh was the first person to enforce the law on the streets.

More than 140 years later, the ASPCA is still enforcing the anticruelty law through its Humane Law Enforcement officers—sometimes called "animal cops"—who investigate complaints and arrest people who are hurting or neglecting their animals. But the ASPCA protects animals in many other ways, too. One of the most important is through its Humane Education department. Humane education means teaching children to care about animals in their own homes and in their communities. It fosters kindness, compassion, and respect for animals, the environment, and other people. Humane education tries to build a sense of responsibility in young people to make the world a better, kinder place.

Here are some exciting ASPCA Humane Education programs to check out.

The **ASPCA Henry Bergh Children's Book Award** (www.aspca.org/bookaward) was set up to honor new books for children and young adults that promote compassion and respect for all living things. Each year the ASPCA gives awards in six categories: Companion Animals, Humane Heroes, Ecology and the Environment, Poetry, Young Adult, and Illustration. It gives separate awards for fiction and nonfiction. Winning books bear the Book Award seal, which consists of a silhouette of a horse and a gentleman wearing a top hat. The awards are named for Henry Bergh because he not only founded the ASPCA to prevent cruelty to animals, but also helped found the New York Society for the Prevention of Cruelty to Children in 1874. It was the first society to protect children from being beaten and starved by their parents. Henry Bergh understood that laws and police powers were not enough to ensure a humane society. Children must be treated kindly and taught to be kind to all living things in turn.

Henry's Book Club (www.aspca.org/henrysbookclub) was formed in 2008 as a way for kids who like animals *and* books to get together to read the ASPCA Henry Bergh Children's Book Award winners and discuss them as a group. Kids meet once a month in clubs that have been organized in schools or communities. The ASPCA provides polls, quizzes, and discussion questions for use at club meetings. Teens over 13 have the option of joining a virtual club through the ASPCA Online Community, where they can chat live about the books with teens across the country—and even with the authors, who join in from time to time as special guests!

ASPCA Kids, Animals, and Literature Bibliography (www.aspca.org/bibliography) is an online list of books about animals that the ASPCA Humane Education staff has reviewed and recommend as accurate, humane, and fun to read. It contains hundreds of titles and is easy to search by subject, title, author, or age, or by whether the book is fiction, nonfiction, or poetry. Winners of the ASPCA Henry Bergh Children's Book Awards are listed, too.

ASPCA Animaland (www.animaland.org) is the ASPCA's interactive web site for kids who love animals. There's a lot to learn at Animaland! Regular features include kids and animals in the news, information about careers working with animals, fun activities, Animal ABCs, and Ask Azula, where ASPCA experts answer kids' questions about animals.

Do Something (www.dosomething.org/aspca) is an online site that gives teens and tweens who want to make a difference lots of information and ideas about how to get involved in issues that matter to them. The ASPCA is the animal welfare partner of Do Something and gives $5,000 worth of grants each year to help fund worthy projects.

Index

A

abandoned horses, 79
adoption, 79
agricultural items, detection dogs for, 18
air-scenting search-and-rescue dogs, 8
alarm dogs, 7
Alaskan Malamute, 34
Alberta Donkey and Mule Club, 73
Algonquin Hotel, New York City, 50–51
Appaloosa, 73
Arlington National Cemetery, 71,
    78–79, 92
arson-detection dogs, 17
ASPCA, 63, 92, 95
Australian Cattle Dog, 5
Australian Shepherd, 5, 9, 25, 28–30

B

barking, 7, 12
barn cat, 40
Bastet, 37
Beagle, 13, 18, 84, 91
Beagle Brigade, 18, 89, 92
Bearded Collie, 9
bedbugs, detection by dogs, 19
Belgian draft horses, 67
Belgian Malinois, 13, 16, 91
Bernese Mountain Dog, 9, 33
blind, guide dogs for the, 24–25, 77, 90
blood donor, 49–50
Bloodhound, 8, 9
bomb detection, 15

Border Collie, 4–5
Budweiser Clydesdales, 64–65, 76, 77–78,
    81, 92
burros, 72
businesses, cats in, 38–39, 49–51

C

Caisson Platoon, U.S. Army, 79
cancer, detection by dogs, 29
Canine Companions for Independence, 26,
    91, 92
care for animals
  companionship, 84
  food, 81–82
  friendship, 83–84
  grooming, 85–87
  rest, 82
  safety, 87–88
  veterinary care, 87
  water, 80–81
cart, pulling by horses, 65–66
cats at work
  entertainment, 47
  as heroes, 46
  hotel cat, 50–51
  in libraries, 41–42
  pest control, 37–40
  retirement, 90
  therapy cats, 43–45, 88
  training cats, 47–48
  in veterinary clinic, 49–51
  in workplaces, 51
Cavalia, 67–68, 92

Clydesdale, 64–65, 76, 77–78, 81
color guard, 60–61
companionship, of working animals, 84
cowboys, 70, 72
crowd control, 14

D

Dachshund, 30–31
dancing horses, 68–69
Delta Society, 32, 92
detection dogs
  arson, 17
  Beagle Brigade, 18, 89, 92
  bedbugs, 19
  bomb, 15
  drug, 13, 15
  food and agricultural items, 18, 89
  health alerts, 29
  mines, 13
  mold, 20
  termites, 19
  truffles, 20
disabled people
  riding programs, 58–59
  service dogs for, 26–29
Doberman Pinscher, 9, 25, 29
dogs at work
  arson detection, 17
  detection work, 13, 15, 17–20
  draft dogs, 33–34
  entertainment, 35
  food and agricultural item detection,
    18, 89

guide dogs, 24–25, 77
herding farm animals, 4–5
military dogs, 12–13
police dogs, 14–16, 89
protecting livestock, 6
retirement, 90–91
search-and-rescue work, 8–9, 88
service dogs, 26–29
sled dogs, 34
therapy dogs, 30–32, 88
watchdogs, 7
water rescue, 10–11
wildlife work, 21
Dog Scouts of America, 11
donkeys, 72
draft dogs, 33–34
draft horses, 63–66
drug detection dogs, 13, 15

E

Egypt, cats in ancient, 37
emotional health assistance, 29
English Shepherd, 5
entertainment, working animals and
  cats, 47
  dogs, 35
  horses, 67–69

F

farm animals. *See* livestock
farrier, 64, 86–87
fires, 17

fleas, 85–86
food
  detection of food items, 18, 89
  use in training, 18, 89
  for working animals, 81–82
Foundation for Pet-Provided Therapy,
    59, 92
friendship, provided by working animals,
    83–84
funerals, use of horses in, 71, 78–79

G

geese, herding, 4
German Shepherd, 7, 13, 16, 21, 25, 29
Golden Retriever, 9, 13, 25, 29
Greater Swiss Mountain Dog, 34
Great Pyrenees, 6
grooming
  cats, 85
  dogs, 85–86
  horses, 86–87
guard dogs, 7
guide dogs, 24–25, 77
Guide Dogs for the Blind, 77, 93
Guide Dogs of America, 90, 92
Guide Horse Foundation, 71, 93
guide horses, 71

H

healing aspects of therapy dogs, 31–32
health alerts, from service dogs, 29
hearing assistance, service dogs for, 28

Helen Woodward Animal Center, 58
herding farm animals, 4–5
heroes, cats as, 46
horses at work
  with cowboys, 70, 72
  draft horses, 63–66
  entertainment, 67–69
  friendship and riding, 54–55
  funerals, 71, 78–79
  guide horses, 71
  park patrol, 56–57
  police horses, 60–62, 78
  retirement, 92
  search-and-rescue, 61, 70–71
  therapy horses, 58–59, 88
hotels, resident cats in, 50–51

I

Icelandic Horse, 56–57, 81, 84
Inn at the Moors, resident cat at, 51
Intermountain Therapy Animals, 93

L

Labrador Retriever, 9, 13, 17, 21,
    25, 29
libraries, cats in, 41–42
Lippizzaner, 68–69, 76
livestock
  herding, 4–5
  protecting, 6
lost people, finding, 8–9
Lusitano, 67, 68

M

Maltese, 32
mental health assistance, 29
messenger dogs, 12–13
military dogs, 12–13, 91
Mill Creek Farm, 91, 93
mine detection dogs, 13
Miniature Horse, 59, 71, 81
Miniature Poodle, 9
mobility assistance, service dogs for, 29
mold, detection by dogs, 20
Morgan Horse, 54–55, 84
motivators, therapy dogs as, 32
mules, 73
mushers, 34

N

National War Dog Monument, 13
Newfoundland, 10–11, 34
Newfoundland Club of America, 11
North American Riding for the
    Handicapped Association, 58–59, 93

P

park patrol horses, 56–57
patrol dogs, 12, 15, 16
Persian cat, 47
pest control, cats and, 37–40
Pit Bull, 9
play, by working animals, 83–84
police dogs, 14–16, 82–83, 89

police horses, 60–62, 78
Pomeranian, 29
predators
    cats as, 37, 38–40
    protecting livestock from, 6
protection
    of livestock, 6
    of property by guard dogs, 7
    of property by police dogs, 14–15

Q

Quarter Horse, 67

R

Ragdoll cat, 50–51
reading programs, 31, 41
rescue groups, 79
rest, for working animals, 82–83
retirement, 90–91
retrieval of items, by service dogs, 29
riding horses, 54–55
Robby's Law, 91
rodent control, by cats, 37–40
Rottweiler, 32, 34
Royal Canadian Mounted Police,
    78, 93

S

safety, of working animals, 87–88, 89
Saint Bernard, 34
Samoyed, 34

San Francisco Society for the Prevention of Cruelty to Animals, 91, 93
scout dogs, 12
search-and-rescue dogs, 8–9, 13, 15, 88
search-and-rescue horses, 61, 70–71
sentry dogs, 12
service dogs
  breeds used as, 29
  emotional/mental health assistance, 29
  examples, 26–28
  health alerts by, 29
  hearing assistance, 28
  mobility assistance, 29
  retrieval of items by, 29
shelters, 76, 79
Shetland Sheepdog, 5
Shih Tzu, 7
Siamese cat, 44–45
Siberian Husky, 34
skijoring, 34
sled dogs, 34, 82
sources of working animals, 76–79
Spanish Mustang, 54
Spanish Riding School, 68–69
Spencer Public Library, 42
Standard Poodle, 9

T

termites, detection by dogs, 19
Texas Hearing and Service Dogs, 79, 93
therapy cats, 43–45, 83
therapy dogs, 30–32, 83
Therapy Dogs International, 32, 93

therapy horses, 58–59
tracking dogs, 8, 21
trail riding, 54
trailing dogs, 8
training
  cats, 47–48
  donkeys, 72
  draft horses, 64, 66
  guide dogs, 25
  horses for entertainment, 68
  ongoing, 89
  police horses, 61–62
  use of food in, 18, 48, 89
truffles, detection by dogs, 20

V

Vest-A-Dog, 93
veterinary care for working animals, 87
veterinary clinic, resident cats in, 49–51

W

watchdogs, 7
water, for working animals, 80–81
water rescue dogs, 10–11
wildlife, dogs working with, 21
wolf, 3
Working Dogs for Conservation Foundation, 21

Y

Yorkshire Terrier, 29